FIRST CORINTHIANS

An Introduction and Study Guide

by
John J. Kilgallen, S.J.

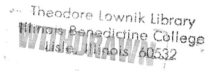

PAULIST PRESS
New York/Mahwah

Artwork and Maps by Frank Sabatté, C.S.P.

Library of Congress Cataloging-in-Publication Data

Kilgallen, John J.
   First Corinthians.

    1. Bible. N.T. Corinthians, 1st—Commentaries.
I. Title. II. Title: 1st Corinthians.
BS2675.3.K55   1986   227'.207   86-20521
ISBN 0-8091-2847-0 (pbk.)

Published by Paulist Press
997 Macarthur Blvd.
Mahwah, N.J. 07430

Printed and bound in the
United States of America

Contents

Introduction

You get on a train at your usual stop; it is the tenth stop the train makes from its starting point. As you enter, you see some people you know, but today you see a number of people who are new to you. Not only do you see them, you hear them, for there is an argument going on (or at least a discussion) and it has obviously been going on for quite some time. You listen, you understand some of it; but you realize that you would understand most all of it if you had been on the train when the argument began. Getting on now is a limitation.

This fictitious story serves to describe the "entry" of a reader who picks up the First Letter to the Corinthians. The reader understands a good deal of what is being said, but soon realizes that he has landed in the midst of something that has roots in the past and which this letter assumes to be known. One has entered, vertically as it were, into a moment which really draws its fuller meaning when it is understood how this moment is the result of many earlier moments. In short, we have Paul's answers to the Corinthians, but what exactly were the questions? We have Paul's correctives, but what exactly was wrong?

This book is an attempt to give something of a better understanding of the problems of the Corinthian Christian community and the circumstances which provoked them; it is also an attempt to make better sense of Paul's answers and approach than one might have from reading the letter for the first time. I say that it is an attempt, because in this situation none of us was present when the Corinthians' train left the station; everyone must try to reconstruct the circumstances which make reading of the letter more understandable and satisfying.

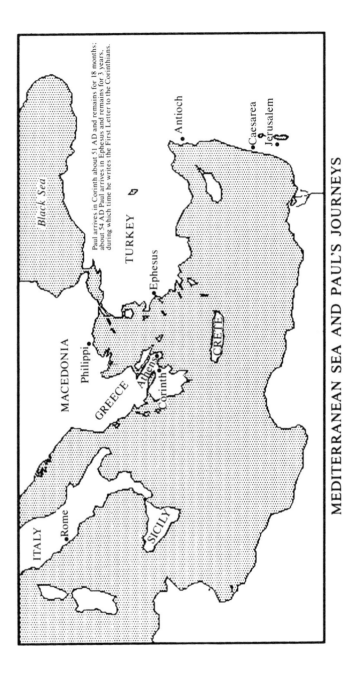

Paul arrives in Corinth about 51 AD and remains for 18 months; about 54 AD Paul arrives in Ephesus and remains for 3 years, during which time he writes the First Letter to the Corinthians.

MEDITERRANEAN SEA AND PAUL'S JOURNEYS

Black Sea

TURKEY

Antioch

Caesarea
Jerusalem

Ephesus

MACEDONIA

Philippi

GREECE

Athens
Corinth

CRETE

ITALY

Rome

SICILY

Scholars have always been convinced that a good picture of the Christian community's life in Corinth is the starting point to enter this Pauline letter. Yet, almost all of the data we can marshal gives a rather imperfect picture and leads us to speculation which, though carefully made, remains speculation. But it is our only available method; so we use it—with caution.

We do not know how many people made up the Corinthian community of Christians at the time this letter was written (presumably about 55–57 A.D.). It is clear from Paul's letter, though, that the community was a cross-section of Corinthian society: some slaves, some wealthy, many ordinary. It is also clear, even from a rapid reading of the letter, that there was in the community a startling variety of approaches to the living out of the baptismal commitment to Christ. For a number of Christians (if Paul is not exaggerating), that a fellow Christian is living in incest causes little disturbance; for some Christians, fornication or prostitution is compatible with their Christianity. A number of the Corinthian Christians have so exalted certain teachers and preachers as to cause deep divisions within the community and incredibly relegated Christ to a level with these men. Some Corinthian Christians cannot accept a resurrection from the dead, especially a physical resurrection, despite what happened in the case of Jesus. Yet, on the other hand, Christians here are inclined to abandon marriage, actual or planned, if Paul gives them the nod; others are erroneously unwilling to eat meat offered to a false god. And it is clear that some Christians of Corinth, by their very bringing of these problems to Paul, take a stance which separates them from others in the community. In short, the Christians of Corinth, though Christian for a rather short time of their lives, are developing ways of living out Christianity which need guidance and control, for too often they not only harm themselves by their misunderstanding but also the community in which they live.

The Corinthians, as they come alive through Paul's letter, are a composite of many viewpoints and moral practices. It is natural to

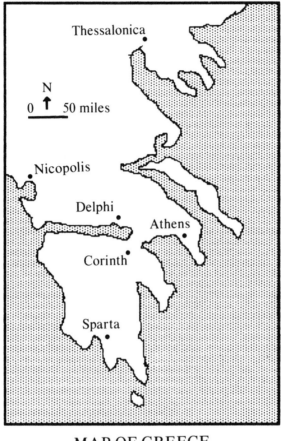

MAP OF GREECE

seek some explanation of the cause of such a variety of views, especially when all call themselves Christians.

Corinth at the Time of Paul

It is difficult to estimate the climate of opinions and viewpoints which swirled about in the Corinth of 55 A.D. To understand this difficulty, one must recall a bit of geography. Corinth itself was situated at the southern end of the neck of land which connected mainland Greece with the Pelopponesus, or southern Greece; in this position, Corinth received everyone who wanted to pass from south to north, from north to south, through Greece. On either side of the neck of land joining northern and southern Greece was a body of water which flowed directly from the Aegean Sea (on the east) and the Adriatic Sea (on the west); since both of these seas connected directly with the Mediterranean Sea, one could say that it was really the whole waterway of the Mediterranean Basin which led to and from the neck of land between northern and southern Greece. Indeed, if one could just dig a canal across this neck of land, one would join the Aegean and Adriatic Seas and make shipping much less precarious than was the case if one had to sail across the big Mediterranean Sea as it spread so awesomely between southern Greece and Africa. Well, there was no canal dug, but ships came to and from the neck of land anyway; at the neck of land they would drop off or pick up goods or be transported across the neck of land to continue their journey through the waters on the other side of the neck. Logically, there was a port placed at each side of the neck of land to receive these ships; one port was called Cenchreae, the other Lechaeon.

Were these two strategic ports independent towns or cities? No, they were both owned by Corinth which sat between them. And one begins to understand the power, vitality and cosmopolitan nature of Corinth; all trade passing on the north-south axis of Greece and the east-west axis from Italy to Turkey, Israel, Egypt and vice versa, passed through Corinth and/or its two ports. We meet this Corinth

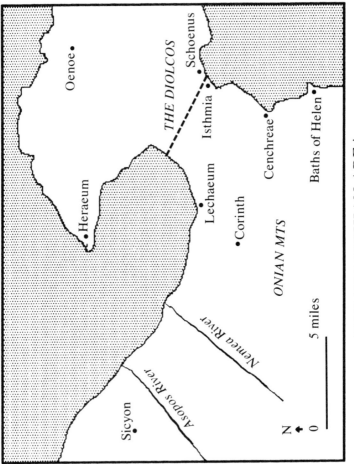

THE CORINTHIAN AREA

about a hundred years after its resurrection by Julius Caesar (it had been destroyed in 146 B.C. and left fallow for a hundred years); it was by Paul's time vigorous and in many ways wealthy, a factor helped by the designation of Corinth as the Roman administrative capital of all Greece.

As can be imagined about such a city as Corinth, all kinds of people passed through it, and many of these chose to stay; indeed, the opportunities for work must have attracted people from all the Mediterranean lands and from lands still beyond those. Included in this mix of people would be Jews who would have a synagogue for themselves and for those Gentiles attracted to Judaism, a synagogue where Paul could begin his preaching about the Jew, Jesus. Here the world-view espoused by the Hebrew scriptures and the traditions of the Jewish interpreters of their scriptures would necessarily meet and react to the ideas, customs, morals, horizons of East and West, North and South. Greece's own heritage of thinking about god, man and happiness continued its own influence within the welter of religions and philosophies that passed through and settled in Corinth.

The Early Christians of Corinth

Since all Corinthian Christians were, as far as we know, adult converts, we can presume that they came to Christianity from lives formed for quite some time according to the mixture of ideas and beliefs each person had absorbed to himself. No doubt a number of these converts were Jewish or acquainted, because of devotion to Judaism, with the thinking and moral patterns of Judaism. But even these would probably have made some adjustments to the culture in which they lived and incorporated some ideas which supported or were akin to their traditions. Given the way in which Judaism in Palestine was divided, though always rooted in the same scriptures, one can understand how, in the wider world, Jews would try to integrate their religion with the culture in which they lived, to the extent that their integrity would allow. This "integration" is no doubt a characteristic of many people, not only Jews, who were to become converts to Christianity; they would bring with them, then, the thoughts and moral behavior which had formed them, as well as their own individual personalities and private approaches to religion. And the integration which was part of their lives in Corinth would, to no one's surprise, continue as they now lived as Christians in the same Corinth. In speaking of "integration" or appropriation of ideas in Corinth, one should be specially aware that not only would a man or woman of substance be converted to Christianity, but with him or her all the household, i.e., servants and slaves; these servants and slaves, full slaves or freemen still paying off the debts they incurred by their being set free—all these were "influenced" both by the thinking of those who owned, cared for and (often) educated them and by the example of the master's conversion. We often read that X became a Christian, he and all his household.

Two aspects or characteristics of life in Corinth are often noted by scholars and so deserve mention here. They are an acute sense of liberty or freedom and a dedication to the fruits of the mind, which is most visibly a dedication to philosophy. These two ideals can fit admirably with Christianity or can be its stiffest opponents. In Corinth there seems to have been a bit of each possibility. At least as some sections of Paul's letter clearly note (6:12 and 10:23), and others imply, there is a heightened sense of individual freedom which does not care very much about the effect it has on the rest of the Christian community. Also, it seems to be a sense of freedom for its own sake as derived from principle, i.e., I am free of all restraints because I am saved. If this be a true representation of the Corinthians, it should be noted that they are not the only ones who drew such a conclusion from a sense of being saved, certainly not the only ones in Corinth itself. But there is a great deal of trust, too, among certain Corinthians in regard to the knowledge the human mind can attain for the sake of happiness, a part of which involves satisfaction of the intellect and guidance by it. Such Corinthians were moved to accept the Christian explanation of forgiveness which leads to happiness, but their innate effort to coordinate their human knowledge and its principles with what faith teaches was at times as aberrant as it was necessary to try. Indeed, often it seems that some Corinthians, left to themselves, tried to keep many of their pre-Christian ideas and fit their new belief in forgiveness and new hope for happiness around them. Some may have thought that, in the last analysis, all they had done was exchange false gods for the true God, a wonderful thing indeed, but an exchange which did not preclude, as far as they could tell on their own, many practices or ideas of their past.

In short, the Corinthians could be addressed as "the holy ones" (1:2), but, upon reading the First Letter to the Corinthians with awareness, one understands how wide a net Paul must use to fit them all under that lofty name. The Corinthians are a mix of many kinds of people; the effort had to be tireless which wanted the response to Christ to be carried out rightly in all areas of life. It falls to Paul to be the tireless worker in this regard, but an appreciation of the Corinthians' tendency to go it their own way will prepare a reader for the fact that Corinthians will be causing trouble for Clement (Pope) in 96 A.D. as they had for Paul in 55 A.D. Evidently the place just encouraged it.

Such, then, is a brief description of the Corinthians; obviously, it is a description owing much to speculation, but to a speculation which tries to explain reasonably the varieties of ways Christianity is practiced in Corinth. What can, what should be said about "the other half" of this letter—St. Paul?

Paul's Background

Paul is a Jew from the diaspora, specifically from Tarsus in present-day southeastern Turkey; though not a native of Palestine, he was extremely loyal to the Old Testament and to the traditions of his elders. Indeed, he could be counted among the most devoted Pharisees, whose outstanding quality was loyalty to Judaism in its fullness; many Pharisees have gone to martyrdom in history. Through

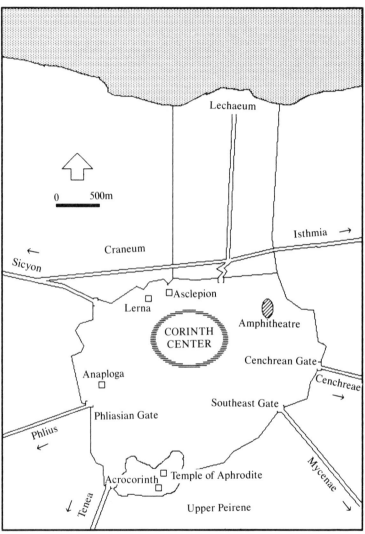

Lechaeum

0   500m

Isthmia →

← Sicyon

Craneum

Asclepion

Lerna

CORINTH CENTER

Amphitheatre

Anaploga

Cenchrean Gate

Cenchreae →

Phliasian Gate

Southeast Gate

← Phlius

Acrocorinth   Temple of Aphrodite

Mycenae →

↓ Tenea

Upper Peirene

THE CITY OF CORINTH

his Phariseeism, Paul grew in the commitment to one God, one God alone, to the resurrection from the dead, to the awareness of sin as the first and ultimate source of unhappiness and death, to the hope he believed God instilled in his chosen people that happiness will be made reachable, to a formidable moral code defining the dignity a human being should attain to be worthy of God. The presence of Christ, then, was the fulfillment of his hopes, the cause of forgiveness of his sins, the model for his own resurrection from the dead, the source of the greatest intimacy mankind has ever known with God, the replacement of the Jewish law as the determinative as to what God thought the dignity of his creature demanded of the creature.

Paul arrived in Corinth for the first time about 51 A.D.; according to the Acts of the Apostles (18:11), Paul remained in Corinth at least eighteen months. Such a lengthy stay must mean that Paul found a good number of Corinthians willing to listen to him and believe what he said. Acts, again, indicates the protection of many in Corinth (implying their conversion?) in the words of the Lord to Paul in a vision: "I am with you. I have so many people on my side here that no harm will come to you" (18:10). Paul, as was his custom, began his preaching in a synagogue there, and found two Jews, Aquila and his wife Priscilla (newly expelled from Rome about 50 A.D. with all other Jews of the capital), with whom Paul became very friendly and worked as tentmaker. When Paul finally upset the Jews of the Corinthian synagogue, he found a Gentile who allowed him room to continue his teaching about Christ. Within this period, then, Paul was able to gather a significant number of Corinthians to the faith in Christ, before he was obliged to move on to preach and teach elsewhere.

Given the atmosphere and tendencies of a city like Corinth, it was not impossible to guess that, once Paul was gone, the Corinthian Christians, left to themselves or under the influence of teachers who presented Jesus a bit differently, would begin to unravel what Paul had so neatly laid out for them. It seems that Paul, before being forced to write what we have come to know as the First Letter to the

Corinthians, wrote at least one letter, and visited Corinth after his writing the First Letter to the Corinthians in order to try again to bring calm to Corinth. With the First Letter to the Corinthians, then, we are caught in the midst of a process in which Paul is being asked to resolve problems and differences and moral practices, some of which he may have inadvertently caused through a teaching which was not totally clear in every detail. What can we say went on in the mind of Paul as he approached this letter-writing?

First, Paul writes out of love and respect for the Corinthians. One can only judge by his words about his love in this letter, but his words of affection for them show no lukewarmness or insincerity. And his record of sacrifices for them, generally spoken of in Chapter 9, are their own witness to this love. Indeed, the final word of his letter is one in which he assures them all that his love is with them. Together with this love comes respect; it is not in irony that he calls them "made holy" (1:2), nor is he insincere in his gratitude to God for "the love of God you have received . . . that you have been enriched in all word and all knowledge" (1:4–5). Too, "the witness to Christ has grown strong among you . . . you are not lacking in any of the gifts of the Spirit" (1:6–7). Indeed, Paul knows himself to be the father of the Corinthian community, a role the obligations of which he never relinquishes; he knows them and treats them "as my beloved children" (4:14).

But the problems of the Corinthians must be acknowledged as serious; incest, misunderstanding about the very essence of Jesus' role in the Corinthian community's salvation and life, doubts about resurrection from the dead, abuse of the Eucharist—these, and other problems as well, demand immediate and concrete solutions.

But not only does the seriousness of the problems weigh on the mind of Paul. One must realize that he sits over two hundred miles away from Corinth and has no practical access to the Corinthians in order to bring their divisiveness and errors to an end by a more personal and immediate presence among them. Paul must simply come up with solutions to very difficult problems through the less satis-

factory form of letter-writing. How much easier, or at least more satisfying, for everyone concerned in these difficulties were Paul able to
meet with those who are acting incorrectly, to discuss and treat de-
licately the personalities and motivations which lay behind and be-
neath the problems. But he is restricted to writing a letter in which
he must try to imagine, after sifting the reports he received, the various states of people in the community, so that he can try to write
effectively.

There is one particular aspect of the mind of Paul which one
must take into consideration with more than ordinary seriousness.
Paul is convinced from his experience in Christ and from his constant
study of the scriptures that the pinnacle of human aspiration and fulfillment is the unity of human beings, supported by the rest of creation, in one great act of worship of the creating and saving God. It
is to this unity that the "great commandments" direct every moment
of life: to love God fully, and to love one's neighbor. The call to oneness, the manner of oneness (in Christ, so that eventually God is all
in all), the removal of barriers or divisions established by human
beings among themselves—all this is the constant teaching of Paul;
it stands as the test of Christianity, as its fulfillment and as its cul-
minating means to happiness. Therefore, it is against Paul's very soul
to see life so lived and decisions so taken, as at Corinth, which reck-
lessly destroy the unity which love so arduously and fragilely builds
and maintains each day. Paul's sensitivity to this call of God to union
determines the energy and decisiveness with which he will respond
to divisiveness and the causes of it. In a word, the preservation of
unity weighs heavily on Paul and enters into the prudential judgments and advice he will give. It is not surprising, therefore, to see
that every one of his decisions in this letter is influenced by what he
thinks will, at least for the time being, maintain the unity of the
community.

But to mention this one concern of Paul is to turn one's attention to the man himself. There is no doubt that, in letter-writing as
in most any other form of communication, the personality of the

writer emerges. This happens in any writing, and will not cease because a certain written work is recognized as the Word of God, the
Sacred Scripture. It is with, apart from or despite the human personality that God makes his contribution and communication to the
reader. One must be able to recognize the distinction between God's
communication and the personality of the human instrument, in order to give proper esteem and respect for God's word.

More concretely, one must be aware that in the case of letter-
writing (Gospel-writing is less subject to this), the personality of the
writer, particularly if it is a strong personality, will be felt. To help
with the reading of Paul's letter, some of his background and makeup should be mentioned so that one understands better the "how"
and the "why" of his writing. I hope that my brevity will not undermine the claim that this is an important investigation.

Paul's Personality

From the fact that Paul was a member of the strictest sect of the
Pharisees and was a tireless and enthusiastic missionary to all kinds
of people throughout the Mediterranean Basin, one can begin to
imagine the type of personality Paul must have had. Add to this that
Paul was recognizably a genius and a most sensitive man in the affairs
of daily living, and one is not caught by surprise to find that he is
determined, energetic, clever, profound, emotional, convinced and
trying to be convincing, argumentative in intellectual matters, decisive and authoritative, attentive and demanding attention, able to
adjust or accommodate himself to circumstances and ideas, but thoroughly washed in the essentials of Judaism, totally committed to
Christ and gifted with the gifts of the Spirit, understanding better
than most all others the implications of Jesus' death and resurrection
so that he sees his life patterned after that double event. He senses
himself to be a leader, the link between Christians and the manner
of living out commitment to Christ. He is an individual able to go
anywhere alone, however fearful he may feel; yet, he longs for union

with God and with all human beings. The Hebrew scriptures and experience are his textbooks about the contours of life into which God has inserted Jesus. He is sensitive to the meaning of sin and forgiveness in a way in which most, even the forgiven and those who search for it, are not; hence, he is grateful to a degree most are not.

It is this person, so strong and so conscientious, so impelled to bring the good news for which centuries have longed and so determined to help make things right (for in the rightness will flower happiness)—it is he, driven to found the Corinthian community, adapting to its every need in order to nourish its growth, who now writes, for want of a more personal visit, to save the community and its members from the effects of their sins and divisiveness and stabilize it once again for the happiness which union with God and neighbor should produce, till the fulfillment of it all when God is all in all.

How will this man write, and what will he write? It is to this we turn as we read and ponder the First Letter to the Corinthians.

STUDY QUESTIONS

1. What kinds of people entered the Christian community at Corinth? How does my own Christian community compare with these early Christians?

2. What kind of city was the Corinth in which Paul planted and nurtured belief in Jesus? How does any city influence the beliefs of Christians?

3. Corinthians loved freedom. Can a love of freedom help people grow to unity? Can it hinder them? How?

4. Corinthians believed in solving problems by use of their minds. How can such a belief be compatible with trust in God and the acceptance of life's answers as "mysteries"?

5. Who is this person Paul? Can one esteem him?

2

The Letter's Beginning

The Greeting (1:1–3)

It is easy to recognize in First Corinthians what are known to be the basic elements of the beginning of a letter of Paul's time—it is the same in all of Paul's letters: the name of the sender is put first, the name of the recipient is placed second, and there follows a wish for continued blessings from God's vigilant love and for peace. Also typical is the way in which all or any of these three basic elements can be embellished; often these embellishments are in themselves of great value in appreciating the Christian mystery. In this letter to the Corinthians, for instance, the Corinthians are characterized as holy, as saints; such description reflects the reality that now human beings (believers in Jesus) can appear in the presence of God without fear of being too unworthy and thus of punishment. This awareness of one's unworthiness to stand in God's presence is a long tradition in Judaism (and in other religions, as well), producing many rites by which a person is cleansed of uncleanness before entering into God's presence. Indeed, even if one could call oneself clean, one should not come closer to God than God himself had indicated. This natural fear and awe of God has now been countered by God himself in that God has, through the instrumentality of Jesus, both cleansed human beings and invited them to the closest intimacy with him; this cleansing and this invitation do not lessen the reality of God which makes him so superior to mankind, but it does show the willingness of God to share an intimacy which most human beings, aware of their unworthiness, find hard to grasp. It is indeed this new relationship which the presence of Jesus confirms; for those who accept him, a life

SCRIPTURE TEXT

1 Paul, called by the will of God to be an apostle of Christ Jesus, and our brother Sos'thenes,

2 To the church of God which is at Corinth, to those sanctified in Christ Jesus, called to be saints together with all those who in every place call on the name of our Lord Jesus Christ, both their Lord and ours:

3 Grace to you and peace from God our Father and the Lord Jesus Christ.

4 I give thanks to God always for you because of the grace of God which was given you in Christ Jesus, [5]that in every way you were enriched in him with all speech and all knowledge— [6]even as the testimony to Christ was confirmed among you— [7]so that you are not lacking in any spiritual gift, as you wait for the revealing of our Lord Jesus Christ; [8]who will sustain you to the end, guiltless in the day of our Lord Jesus Christ. [9]God is faithful, by whom you were called into the fellowship of his Son, Jesus Christ our Lord.

of intimacy with God is the reality—and this "worthiness" to be with him is holiness, sanctity.

Another embellishment of the typical elements of the greeting format is Paul's effort to make the Corinthians aware of their unity with all those who have called on the name of Jesus, i.e., with all those who have accepted Jesus as their Lord. These elements—the centrality of Jesus and the sense of unity—are vital to the body of Paul's letter and represent two of the pillars on which Christianity is built. Particularly in regard to unity, anyone of Paul's Jewish (not to mention Pharisaic) background, totally influenced by the theology of the Hebrew scriptures, knows that the original (and still existing) plan of God for his creation presumed as essential the unity of all created beings, in a unity with God. With this unity pushed aside, there is no Judaism, there is no Christianity, there is no understanding of the mind of God for creation; everything becomes a jumble of unintelligibility.

The Thanksgiving (1:4–9)

Another typical element of a letter written in Paul's time (and used in most of Paul's letters) is a thanksgiving; it is a moment in which the writer expresses gratitude for any number of things, compressed under the title of "good news about those to whom he writes." In the thanksgiving of First Corinthians, Paul is grateful for the myriad ways he knows and hears in which God sheds his love on the Corinthians. This continual flow of God's love is recognized by Paul particularly as visible in three ways: in the enrichment of the Corinthians through those who have preached and taught in Corinth, a subject Paul will take up with the Corinthians in a few moments, in the ability to witness strongly to Christ and in the gifts of the Spirit poured out on the Corinthians because of their belief in Christ, subjects to be developed specifically as the letter proceeds. We also learn from this thanksgiving how central to early Christianity was the "waiting" for Jesus to return, to take his own with him to heaven—and the Corinthians will persevere to this day, for God, who has done so much for them, will continue faithful to them to the end. While using the typical thanksgiving element in letter-writing, then, Paul has given broad indications of the life of the community committed to Jesus and of its wait for him, assured by the love of God; he has also suggested the importance of unity, of Jesus, of the gifts of the Spirit, of the love of God—elements which need to be addressed seriously in this letter, for they are not well understood by the Corinthians. Indeed, one could say that, though Paul is rendering thanks as one might expect in a first-century letter, he is already preaching, encouraging, teaching the Corinthians the basic elements he knows they need to be true to Christianity.

STUDY QUESTIONS

1. What does Paul mean by calling Christians "holy," "Saints"?

2. What makes "unity" such an essential charateristic of Judaism/Christianity?

3. For what thing is Paul grateful when he thinks of the Corinthians? How do these things define the way a Christian thinks about life with God?

4. In what ways can Paul be said already to be "preaching, encouraging, teaching" in the Greeting and Thanksgiving sections of his letter?

3

First Problem:
The Divisions within
the Corinthian Church (1:10–4:21)

The key to understanding the wealth of material Paul gives in Chapters 1:10–4:21 is the list of four slogans which sum up the situation reported to him by "Chloe's people" (Corinthians who gathered, probably, at the house of a Corinthian Christian lady, Chloe): "I am Paul's," "I am Apollos'," "I am Cephas'," "I am Christ's." These slogans indicated to Paul a division of the Corinthian church into factions, and such a division as to thoroughly rend the entire fabric of the community. Moreover, these slogans manifest the profound misunderstanding of how Jesus relates to every Christian and to all Christians together, and how Jesus relates to Paul, Apollos, Cephas. From Paul's point of view, in which Christ plays the central and unique role of savior, to assign Christ to any position other than the center of Christian life is to ruin the very reality Jesus, he believes, came to create.

How does Paul try to correct the erroneous understanding these slogans so sadly announce? He does this in four ways. First, he reasserts the centrality of Jesus and him crucified (1:13a). Second, he recalls each Corinthian's baptism as a "baptism in his name" (1:13b). Third, he argues, in a way of thinking that appeals to the Corinthians, that the meaning of Jesus crucified is the only true wisdom (1:17–2:16; 3:18–23). Fourth, Paul sets forth the true relationship that should exist between Jesus and Christian preachers; within this fourth presentation, Paul eventually touches upon personal elements

SCRIPTURE TEXT

10 I appeal to you, brethren, by the name of our Lord Jesus Christ, that all of you agree and that there be no dissensions among you, but that you be united in the same mind and the same judgment. [11]For it has been reported to me by Chlo'e's people that there is quarreling among you, my brethren. [12]What I mean is that each one of you says, "I belong to Paul," or "I belong to Apol'los," or "I belong to Cephas," or "I belong to Christ." [13]Is Christ divided? Was Paul crucified for you? Or were you baptized in the name of Paul? [14]I am thankful that I baptized none of you except Crispus and Ga'ius; [15]lest any one should say that you were baptized in my name. [16](I did baptize also the household of Steph'anas. Beyond that, I do not know whether I baptized any one else.) [17]For Christ did not send me to baptize but to preach the gospel, and not with eloquent wisdom, lest the cross of Christ be emptied of its power.

18 For the word of the cross is folly to those who are perishing, but to us who are being saved it is the power of God. [19]For it is written,

"I will destroy the wisdom of the wise,
and the cleverness of the clever I will thwart.'"

[20]Where is the wise man? Where is the scribe? Where is the debater of this age? Has not God made foolish the wisdom of the world? [21]For since, in the wisdom of God, the world did not know God through wisdom, it pleased God through the folly of what we preach to save those who believe. [22]For Jews demand signs and Greeks seek wisdom, [23]but we preach Christ crucified, a stumbling block to Jews and folly to Gentiles, [24]but to those who are called, both Jews and Greeks, Christ the power of God and the wisdom of God. [25]For the foolishness of

God is wiser than men, and the weakness of God is stronger than men.

26 For consider your call, brethren; not many of you were wise according to worldly standards, not many were powerful, not many were of noble birth; [27]but God chose what is foolish in the world to shame the wise, God chose what is weak in the world to shame the strong, [28]God chose what is low and despised in the world, even things that are not, to bring to nothing things that are, [29]so that no human being might boast in the presence of God. [30]He is the source of your life in Christ Jesus, whom God made our wisdom, our righteousness and sanctification and redemption; [31]therefore, as it is written, "Let him who boasts, boast of the Lord."

2 When I came to you, brethren, I did not come proclaiming to you the testimony of God in lofty words or wisdom. [2]For I decided to know nothing among you except Jesus Christ and him crucified. [3]And I was with you in weakness and in much fear and trembling; [4]and my speech and my message were not in plausible words of wisdom, but in demonstration of the Spirit and power, [5]that your faith might not rest in the wisdom of men but in the power of God.

6 Yet among the mature we do impart wisdom, although it is not a wisdom of this age or of the rulers of this age, who are doomed to pass away. [7]But we impart a secret and hidden wisdom of God, which God decreed before the ages for our glorification. [8]None of the rulers of this age understood this; for if they had, they would not have crucified the Lord of glory. [9]But, as it is written,

> "What no eye has seen, nor ear heard,
> nor the heart of man conceived,
> what God has prepared for those who
> love him,"

[10]God has revealed to us through the Spirit. For the Spirit

searches everything, even the depths of God. [11]For what person knows a man's thoughts except the spirit of the man which is in him? So also no one comprehends the thoughts of God except the Spirit of God. [12]Now we have received not the spirit of the world, but the Spirit which is from God, that we might understand the gifts bestowed on us by God. [13]And we impart this in words not taught by human wisdom but taught by the Spirit, interpreting spiritual truths to those who possess the Spirit.

14 The unspiritual man does not receive the gifts of the Spirit of God, for they are folly to him, and he is not able to understand them because they are spiritually discerned. [15]The spiritual man judges all things, but is himself to be judged by no one. [16]"For who has known the mind of the Lord so as to instruct him?" But we have the mind of Christ.

3 But I, brethren, could not address you as spiritual men, but as men of the flesh, as babes in Christ. [2]I fed you with milk, not solid food; for you were not ready for it; and even yet you are not ready, [3]for you are still of the flesh. For while there is jealousy and strife among you, are you not of the flesh, and behaving like ordinary men? [4]For when one says, "I belong to Paul," and another, "I belong to Apol'los," are you not merely men?

5 What then is Apol'los? What is Paul? Servants through whom you believed, as the Lord assigned to each. [6]I planted, Apol'los watered, but God gave the growth. [7]So neither he who plants nor he who waters is anything, but only God who gives the growth. [8]He who plants and he who waters are equal, and each shall receive his wages according to his labor. [9]For we are fellow workers for God; you are God's field, God's building.

10 According to the commission of God given to me, like a skilled master builder I laid a foundation, and another man is building upon it. Let each man take care how he builds upon it. [11]For no other foundation can any one lay than

that which is laid, which is Jesus Christ. [12]Now if any one builds on the foundation with gold, silver, precious stones, wood, hay, stubble—[13]each man's work will become manifest; for the Day will disclose it, because it will be revealed with fire, and the fire will test what sort of work each one has done. [14]If the work which any man has built on the foundation survives, he will receive a reward. [15]If any man's work is burned up, he will suffer loss, though he himself will be saved, but only as through fire.

16 Do you not know that you are God's temple and that God's Spirit dwells in you? [17]If any one destroys God's temple, God will destroy him. For God's temple is holy, and that temple you are.

18 Let no one deceive himself. If any one among you thinks that he is wise in this age, let him become a fool that he may become wise. [19]For the wisdom of this world is folly with God. For it is written, "He catches the wise in their craftiness," [20]and again, "The Lord knows that the thoughts of the wise are futile." [21]So let no one boast of men. For all things are yours, [22]whether Paul or Apol′los or Cephas or the world or life or death or the present or the future, all are yours; [23]and you are Christ's; and Christ is God's.

4 This is how one should regard us, as servants of Christ and stewards of the mysteries of God. [2]Moreover it is required of stewards that they be found trustworthy. [3]But with me it is a very small thing that I should be judged by you or by any human court. I do not even judge myself. [4]I am not aware of anything against myself, but I am not thereby acquitted. It is the Lord who judges me. [5]Therefore do not pronounce judgment before the time, before the Lord comes, who will bring to light the things now hidden in darkness and will disclose the purposes of the heart. Then every man will receive his commendation from God.

6 I have applied all this to myself and Apol′los for your benefit, brethren, that you may learn by us to live according to scripture, that none of you may be puffed up in favor of one against another. ⁷For who sees anything different in you? What have you that you did not receive? If then you received it, why do you boast as if it were not a gift?

8 Already you are filled! Already you have become rich! Without us you have become kings! And would that you did reign, so that we might share the rule with you! ⁹For I think that God has exhibited us apostles as last of all, like men sentenced to death; because we have become a spectacle to the world, to angels and to men. ¹⁰We are fools for Christ's sake, but you are wise in Christ. We are weak, but you are strong. You are held in honor, but we in disrepute. ¹¹To the present hour we hunger and thirst, we are ill-clad and buffeted and homeless, ¹²and we labor, working with our own hands. When reviled, we bless; when persecuted, we endure; ¹³when slandered, we try to conciliate; we have become, and are now, as the refuse of the world, the offscouring of all things.

14 I do not write this to make you ashamed, but to admonish you as my beloved children. ¹⁵For though you have countless guides in Christ, you do not have many fathers. For I became your father in Christ Jesus through the gospel. ¹⁶I urge you, then, be imitators of me. ¹⁷Therefore I sent to you Timothy, my beloved and faithful child in the Lord, to remind you of my ways in Christ, as I teach them everywhere in every church. ¹⁸Some are arrogant, as though I were not coming to you. ¹⁹But I will come to you soon, if the Lord wills, and I will find out not the talk of these arrogant people but their power. ²⁰For the kingdom of God does not consist in talk but in power. ²¹What do you wish? Shall I come to you with a rod, or with love in a spirit of gentleness?

which connect him intimately to the Corinthians and uses them as motivation to urge the Corinthians to change their ways (3:1–4:21). Let us discuss each of these four points, in the order in which Paul presents them.

1. The Centrality of Jesus Crucified

More than once in these four chapters Paul insists on the centrality of Jesus crucified. His very first retorts to the slogans raise the question of crucifixion, as though knowledge of who died for the Corinthians should instantly destroy the slogans (and the allegiances and divisions they signify) and replace them with one slogan, one allegiance, and with unity. Why is Jesus crucified the key to the Corinthians' problem?

To Jesus crucified is owed by every believer an incalculable debt. The human race had been in "down-cycle" from the moment of Adam's sin, a sin which introduced the penalty which befit sin, i.e., the penalty of death. Every human being, human experience makes perfectly clear, shares in the radical termination of life, and this termination of life is ascribed to the sin of Adam and to the subsequent sins of each human being. Sin, one must understand in this context, is the conscious separation from the source of life; one cannot expect to continue in life if one has turned one's back on the source of life. To distance oneself from God is to lose contact with life; though not intentionally so, it is a choice of death. It matters little to this discussion that one can distinguish between mortal and venial sin, between grave sin and less serious sin; what is visible to all is that we all die, and the cause of this lamentable termination is, according to the scriptures, the inherent, natural, necessary and immediate result of the rejection of God we call sin.

Such, then, is the human situation, and such it remains no matter how firmly human achievements push back the hands of death which reach out for us continually. Nothing human beings can do can mitigate the punishment for sin, nor delay it unduly. Corruption is now our fate, a corruption which lasts as long as does the will act which separates us from Life. It is a corruption, a death, which lasts forever.

There is only one way by which eternal death can be avoided, even eliminated; God must forgive the sins which make us die. And this forgiveness must be freely given, in the sense that human beings can never do enough to make up for sin and thus oblige God to forgive, as though we had paid our debt and deserved pardon. So all eyes turn to the One who, though continually spurned by mankind, offers the only hope of terminating eternal death. What will he do?

What God chose to do in this situation was not foreseeable, though Paul and others felt that the Old Testament had offered hints of God's intention for man's benefit. From hindsight, after the crucifixion of Jesus, Paul realized what God had actually done to reverse the irreversible situation into which human beings had gotten themselves. What Paul grasped from the fact of Jesus' death and subsequent resurrection can be laid out in at least three points.

First, God did not choose simply to ignore the punishment due to sins; he insisted that the only way he would forgive guilt and its effects was not by ignoring death, but by having someone experience it. Thus, death was not avoided and sin was paid for in the coinage it naturally demanded; sin was not forgiven and forgotten, until it had been paid for by the price it of itself demanded.

Second, God, though demanding that the penalty for sin be experienced, did not ask that the horror of eternal death be experienced. In this the merciful love of God is revealed. He asked for the terrible pain of human dissolution, but unilaterally and freely brushed aside what is the natural characteristic of death due to sin: an eternal corruption.

Third, not only did God limit the penalty to be suffered to a "moment" of tortured corruption; he asked this suffering from the one person who did not deserve it, who did nothing to merit the punishment reserved to those who turn away from God. Thus, not only is an essential characteristic of death, its eternality, waived, but the guilty are not the ones who have to pay whatever suffering God asks for the forgiveness of sins. The innocent suffers so that the guilty go free.

But the richest understanding of what God chose to do for human beings irreversibly headed for eternal death involves the perception of who this innocent one is who suffers for the guilty. Once one realizes that the suffering of death is asked, not simply of a human being, but of the Son of God, then one understands, however imperfectly, that God himself is undertaking the penalty of death which guilty mankind deserves. One can (and scripture does) distinguish carefully and really between the Father and his Son; but even with this distinction in mind, the reparation of sin remains in the divine family as it lovingly looks to the needs of creatures. It is, then, from within God himself that the act comes whereby those who deserve death are set free. Jesus' death is this divine experience of the penalty which should have been experienced by human beings.

Through the death of Jesus, then, God has reversed the fate of all human beings. This act of Jesus allows us to have what no one else could give us. He alone has offered human beings the chance for eternal happiness. Why, then, is a Paul or an Apollos or a Cephas preferred to him, or considered the center of one's life? What did any of them do to reverse the irreversible? If one depends on them, as the slogans seem to suggest, one can only expect to remain dead forever; these men are useless in one's most significant need.

It is possible that a Corinthian, in self-defense, might say that we (and Paul before us) have misunderstood the significance of the slogans. The harsh understanding of them and the one we have followed implies that the Corinthians have preferred this or that preacher to Jesus. A milder interpretation would be that Jesus is always at the center of every Corinthian life (despite what the slogans suggest), but each Corinthian has chosen what he thinks to be the most appealing Jesus. That is, Apollos may well have emphasized a Jesus who, like the Greek and Roman philosophers, taught the principles by which one's life could be truly happy. Cephas might have stressed the miraculous powers of Jesus as signs of that power which can save us totally. Those who championed "the Christ" might have emphasized a Jesus who was sent to save in accordance with the prophecies of the Old Testament as a second David or a new Moses or a more perfect Elijah. But even if such an interpretation be the truth behind the slogans, these are not the images or aspects of Jesus which stand at the core of his unique relationship to mankind; indeed, if these aspects of Jesus are not understood well and integrated into the reality of Jesus crucified, they can be a hindrance to the full truth of Jesus as representing and revealing the Father. Again, Paul points to the crucified Jesus as the true core of the Christian's life of hope, and of the entire Christian community.

2. Baptism in the Name of Jesus

But not only does Paul respond to the slogans by an immediate reference to Jesus crucified; he also reminds the Corinthians that they were baptized in Jesus' name alone. Why does he refer to this baptism in the name of Jesus? He does this simply to remind the Corinthians that in every case of baptism it was in the name of Jesus, not in that of Paul or Apollos or Cephas, that the baptism was performed. And what did baptism in his name mean? First, it meant a belief in all that the cross revealed and stood for; it meant belief that Jesus was the one (and only one) through whom happiness was now possible. Second, it meant an acceptance of Jesus, now alive, as one's Lord; concretely, this "acceptance of Jesus as Lord" meant an obedience to the way of life he indicated as the way in which love of God and love of neighbor is carried out. Third, and perhaps most profoundly, baptism means actually sharing in that source of life which enlivened Jesus at his resurrection. Because this sharing of the one source of life (so that one can say that he shares the risen life of Jesus) is so intimate, one has the power, the strength that flows from this life-source; one actually begins to live a life of God and with God, with the accom-

panying strength of one alive. Hence, one is able, strong enough to
live in love of God and neighbor. And one can do this because one
shares the life-source by which Jesus lives; one is in him. Baptism,
then, is totally taken up with Jesus, and not with a Paul or an Apollos
or a Cephas; from none of them does one share in the life which sup-
ports the effort to love.

But not only does baptism serve as the action by which one formally acknowledges the supreme gift Jesus gave mankind by his
death and commits oneself to the Lordship of Jesus and to the belief
that he shares in the very source of life by which Jesus now lives;
baptism is also a public profession of belief that the motive of Jesus'
dying, love of God, which brought death to a halt and issued in life
with God, is the supreme motive of the Christian's life. Jesus becomes the model not only because the Christian hopes to look like
him someday (i.e., be risen from the dead), but because the Christian
knows that the way to resurrection is the way exemplified by Jesus
in all aspects of his life, but singularly in his freely accepting death
out of love for God and mankind. Baptism, then, is a most significant action, but, more importantly for the argument of Paul, it has
all its significance in relation only to Jesus; no other human being
gives any meaning to baptism.

Paul hopes to correct the errors of the Corinthian slogans by
recalling the death of Jesus and the formal moment of the Corinthians' acceptance of all that that death and the consequent resurrection
meant; in the light of this, Jesus can be seen as the sole center of the
Christian experience and of the community which results from it.

3. *Wisdom and Foolishness*

The third endeavor in understanding the fullness of Paul's answer to the Corinthian slogans is to come to grips with the framework
of "wisdom" and "foolishness" which characterizes so much of the
first two chapters of the letter (and 3:18–23, as well). Specifically,

why did Paul choose to interpret the death of Jesus in terms of "wisdom" and "foolishness"? And what does it mean to say that the death of Jesus is "wisdom"? Let us answer the first question first.

Every culture has its approach to the problem of securing human happiness. The contribution Greece made to this endeavor is this, that it is the human mind, used to understand self, nature and society, that is the premiere tool to achieve happiness. A tribute to this trust in the mind is the continued education, built on the conviction of the Greeks, that we employ today; though one can study for the sheer pleasure of learning, the deepest value of learning is the securing of happiness. By understanding, then, one becomes wise, one grows in the ability to discern the good from the bad, the wise way from the foolish way of life. One associates this discernment with the philosophers of Greece because they were the ones who tried to grasp the teachings of all the arts and sciences in a unity which most surely leads to happiness.

It is difficult to say how much the individual Corinthian of Paul's Christian community sought happiness in terms of wisdom and foolishness; this is especially problematic in that over half the people living in Corinth probably were not native Greeks and thus did not "inherit" the Greek way of looking at things. How many of the Corinthian Christians were native Corinthians is unknown. Yet, there must have been enough of the Greek tradition felt in the Corinthian community to warrant Paul's speaking of Jesus' death in terms of "wisdom" and "foolishness"; probably Paul knew enough of the influence of this way of thinking from his own personal experience in Corinth where he stayed for over eighteen months (cf. Acts 18:11).

What would the "wise" man, who uses his mind to overcome the obstacles to happiness, say about the death of Jesus as the unique means to ultimate happiness? To formulate the question is to suggest its answer. On the face of it, it looks as though Jesus got caught in the same web of corruption as any other human being, and even more ingloriously; instead of coming up with the wisdom to avoid the greatest threat to happiness, i.e., death, he died. Can that be the mark of the wisdom which leads to the fullest happiness? Paul admits, of course, that one must understand the death of Jesus properly, but he also acknowledges that this "proper understanding" is itself a gift, given to those "on the way to salvation." He suggests then that, left to itself, the human mind, the Greek's best tool to happiness, will only be confused by the suggestion that Jesus' death is the key to human happiness. Unless the Spirit of God—which, like the spirit of any person, is the only one who really knows the innermost depths—unless this Spirit communicates the innermost thoughts of God and their meaning, the Greek will never understand how the death of Jesus is saving; he will call it all foolishness.

In an analogous way, the death of Jesus in the eyes of a Jew is senseless as a means of salvation. For the Jew, the traditional means of God's salvation, as evidenced over and over again in the Hebrew scriptures, is the exercise of divine power by which Israel is saved from its enemies. Every step of Israel's success, from its miraculous beginning in Abraham to its glory under King Solomon, is chronicled as the effect of God's loving, miraculous intervention on Israel's behalf. In the light of this pattern of divine wonder-working as the means to save Israel, how does Jesus crucified fit the pattern? Unless one has the guidance of God's own Spirit, who can alone make sense of this impotent Jesus, who sets no example by which to escape oppression, humiliation at the hands of one's enemies, death—unless one is guided by the Spirit, one will not accept the death of Jesus as a saving from one's worst enemies.

But Paul is dealing primarily at Corinth with the Greek ways of achieving happiness, and so his argument is heavily in terms of true wisdom and true foolishness. One way Paul has of demonstrating his point, that the cross of Jesus is the true wisdom leading to happiness, is to ask the Corinthians to consider themselves for a moment. Briefly put, they have nothing of the wherewithal which the world considers necessary means to achieve happiness; thus, as far as the judgment of the world is concerned, they are judged foolish—

they will never walk the "right" path, the "wise" path leading to happiness. Yet, the Corinthians know that they are already justified in God's eyes, reconciled with the one with whom one must either be reconciled or fail to reach happiness; they know that they have in great measure done what is necessary to achieve the happiness for which the world seeks. And they know that they have progressed so far because of the death of Jesus and their embracing it, the very death both Jew and Greek reject as impotent and foolish. Thus, the Corinthians, foolish in the eyes of the world's wisdom, are really wise because, if anybody is going to reach happiness, it is they—because they have embraced Jesus crucified. They turn out to be the truly wise; their critics are the truly foolish.

So, the cross is explained in terms of wisdom and foolishness, terms which are the framework in which the Corinthians do their divisive boasting. However wrong the Corinthians show themselves to be in regard to the question of the centrality of Jesus crucified, Paul is clearly disturbed by the added wrong that all their views are wrapped in a claim to wisdom which is terribly false and a sure injustice to the concept of true wisdom. Whatever the merits of human reasoning about happiness and of human persuasion based on that reasoning by the human mind, unless one grasps the reality that God's wisdom, his mysteries, "what is beyond the mind of man," the truest wisdom—unless one grasps this, indeed is helped to grasp it, the mind will fail ultimately to lead a person to the happiness for which one longs. Without understanding and believing what God accomplished for mankind through Jesus' death, one will never know the elements which are essential to salvation and happiness; but without that knowledge, one is foolish and cannot begin to reach out for the happiness for which he is destined.

4. *Jesus and the Role of Christian Preachers*

Having established Jesus crucified as the one assurance of ultimate happiness, Paul spends a good deal of time, through Chapters

3 and 4, defining and explaining the role played by the Corinthians' teachers and preachers, those men of the slogans: Cephas, Apollos and Paul. Paul begins by suggesting a variety of images by which to understand these men better.

First, there is the depiction of Paul and Apollos as servants who brought the message to which the Corinthians have responded. Then, they are described as co-workers with God; in this image there is recognition of the different ways in which the co-workers with God worked (Paul planting, Apollos watering), as well as of the essential role of God who alone makes the plants grow. Third, they are those who build on the foundation which is Jesus, and they must be careful how they build on this foundation lest they build poorly; if, in the purifying fire at the end time, their work does not stand up to the purifying test, they will lose any reward they might have earned for their laborious preaching and teaching. Indeed, considering that the community is not just any building but the temple of God in which dwells the Holy Spirit, one can see why any preacher or teacher who does not build this temple well will be punished severely. Finally, Paul describes the preachers as Christ's servants, his stewards entrusted with the message of salvation. Thus, there is a clear distinction between the essential, central position of Jesus in the community and the supportive role of the preachers and teachers who labor to ever enhance the significance of Jesus in the community.

These images, then, give some idea of the serious need to put the preachers and teachers into a category absolutely distinct from Jesus. But having made this distinction through much of these first four chapters of his letter, Paul now subtly interposes a second distinction; this time, the distinction rests between Paul and all the other preachers and teachers. What kind of distinction is this? What is its basis?

Paul's Special Relationship with the Corinthian Church

It is near the end of Chapter 4 that Paul brings forth the image of the "guardian" (v. 15). The guardian was a person of maturity who did for the children of a family just about all the things they needed for their upbringing; the guardian was responsible for preparing the little child for school, for taking him there and bringing him back home, for watching over his lessons, etc. Clearly, the guardian had a great deal of influence over the child, and the child owed much to the guardian. And yet, for all that that relationship might mean, it cannot compare in importance with the relationship between father and child. And it is to the importance and centrality of father that Paul appeals for a right image of himself vis-à-vis the Corinthians. While there may be many, even "a thousand" guardians whom the Corinthians can gratefully identify, they must acknowledge Paul as their one father who gave them life, who brought them into the reality of blessed Christianity. No doubt, then, that Paul, Apollos, Cephas and countless others are completely secondary to Jesus; but a peek into that crowded category of teachers and preachers will reveal one who stands before all others: Paul, the father of the Corinthian Christians. Paul wants his fatherhood clearly recognized.

But why does Paul "wear his heart on his sleeve"? Though he realizes the snub the slogans clearly offer him, it is not simply to regain the favor and love of the Corinthians which he, their father, deserves. More than to eliminate his hurt, Paul acts to re-establish his right to be heard, above all others, as to what the Christian mystery is all about. Paul is not so much motivated by a desire to own the approval of the Corinthians, as he is by the terrible anxiety with which he sees crumbling before him the foundation of Christian life and the unity it should naturally create.

Paul at this point has entered more clearly than before onto the personal level. He appeals to his principal role in founding the Corinthian community as a reason for the Corinthians' paying attention to him rather than to others. He had earlier insisted that he had nothing to apologize for, despite the judgments of others; he has nothing on his conscience in regard to his relations with the Corinthians. He is ready to challenge those who claim to know more about Christianity than he; the challenge will not be in the area of rhetoric, but in regard to power, for it is in the doing, the expressing of love, that true wisdom proves itself. Finally, Paul asks that the Corinthians imitate him, copy him; the goal is unity and Paul knows that the love which produced so much good at Corinth is a model that the Corinthians can follow with success.

In his attempt to reassert his leadership in interpreting the mystery of Christianity, Paul not only argues that he is the "father" of the Corinthian community, the one "who planted," the one "who laid the foundation." He also takes the Corinthians to task for the pride which he sees standing behind their willingness to spurn other Christians in their holding fast to their "wisdom." Part of the cause of the dissension in Corinth is, Paul strongly implies, the haughtiness which is content with division and is insensitive to the loveless situation "wisdom" has caused. Known by its fruits, true wisdom does not end in factions and satisfaction with disunity, but in love. The Corinthians' claim to wisdom, therefore, is a false claim; theirs is a "wisdom" which produced only the results of real foolishness. And they must not only regain the true wisdom of Jesus crucified, but be humble enough to love.

Wisdom and the Holy Spirit

As we come to the end of this discussion of Paul's first four chapters, one might pause for a moment to reflect on two points which are in some way consequences of Paul's remarks about wisdom and foolishness. First, through the centuries Christians have on occasion understood St. Paul here to condemn all human wisdom; and if he has not condemned it, he has suggested that Christians be suspicious of it. Second, St. Paul has here contributed to the difficulty raised in other New Testament works concerning the ability of a human mind to "come to God" without God's aid; to cite a more explicit statement pertinent to this matter, the Gospel of John notes that "No one can come to me unless he is drawn by the Father who sent me" (Jn 6:44). St. Paul's own suggestion is in terms of the Holy Spirit: " 'The things that no eye has seen and no ear heard, things beyond the mind of man' . . . these are the very things that God has revealed to us through the Spirit . . . we have received the Spirit that comes from God to teach us to understand the gifts he has given us. . . . An unspiritual person [i.e., a person without the Spirit] is one who does not accept anything of the Spirit of God; he sees it all as nonsense and it is beyond his understanding because it can be understood only by means of the Spirit" (2:9–14). Both these points deserve some brief comment.

It is true that, in this letter, Paul ridicules human wisdom: "Where are any of our thinkers today? Do you not see how God has shown up the foolishness of human wisdom?" (1:20). But one must be clear as to the grounds on which he makes this criticism. Specifically, Paul finds fault with the human wisdom that does not lead to God, that tries to replace him, and that does not issue in love. Paul's words do not really allow one to conclude that he sees no value in human thinking, human study; what he is dealing with is a situation in which human beings have come up with ways to salvation which ignore the one, true way, and it is in ridicule of this kind of wisdom that Paul speaks. In short, he has nothing to say here about the integration of the human mind's pursuit of happiness with the divine plan or wisdom, except to imply that they should fit together (somehow) and not have the former toss aside the latter. Actually, it is not Paul who introduces the idea of criticizing "wisdom"; the slogans of the Corinthians already suggest such ridicule. Paul is trying to combat their notions of wisdom by identifying the true wisdom. To the extent that they substitute their wisdom for that of God, to that extent they are wrong; Paul never discusses human wisdom as it refers to problems outside that of salvation.

As for the second effect of Paul's words in 1 Corinthians 1–4, it is clear that he highlights two points. First, there are things hidden in God which the human mind cannot reach until God reveals them. Second, if one remains unspiritual, i.e., without God's Holy Spirit, one will not make sense of what God reveals. In the one case, human wisdom, whatever be the good will which inspires it, will never learn the truth unless God wills it; in the other case, only if one has the inner disposition necessary for hearing the Spirit will the Spirit's words of revelation be heard. Thus, one may be considered wise, yet be unable (or be no longer able) to comprehend God's wisdom simply because one is not favorable to the influence of the Spirit. And one of the most significant elements of this interaction between a human being and the Spirit of God is the conviction of Paul, and of the New Testament, that even to be favorably disposed to hearing and understanding the Spirit is, itself, a gift of the Spirit; thus, the willingness to hear favorably the revelation freely given by God is not without the help of God, freely given. Before this mystery, in which man is responsible for his attentiveness to the Spirit, yet dependent on the Spirit for this very attentiveness, Paul's anxiousness about the Corinthians becomes more understandable: having been moved by the Spirit to accept baptism and the gift of the Spirit associated with baptism, are they now to turn a deaf ear to the Spirit who makes sense of the death of Jesus, in favor of human guidance to happiness? If they do, will the gift freely given and now spurned be freely given again?

Whether or not what Paul tackles as the first problem of the Corinthian community was the first complaint he received about the young Corinthian church, it serves as a fitting starting point for his letter to them; for it is only by understanding and accepting the central place of Jesus in the Christian's life and in the life of the community that the church of Corinth is set on its proper foundation. Other problems, some of a less serious nature to be sure, may now be discussed, for the essential grounding of Christian unity has been reaffirmed.

STUDY QUESTIONS

1. Describe the first problem Paul addresses. What are the implications of saying that "I am Apollos'," etc.?

2. How does Paul argue that everyone should say only, "I belong to Jesus"?

3. Why is Jesus crucified so important for Paul? What did Paul grasp from the fact of Jesus' death and resurrection?

4. Why did Paul refer to baptism in order to argue that Jesus alone is central to a Christian's faith?

5. Why are the terms "wisdom" and "power," used by Paul about Jesus crucified? Why is Jesus' death "wise," why is it "foolish"? Why is his death "weakness," why is it "strength"?

6. What are the true roles Apollos, Cephas and Paul play in relation to Jesus' role?

7. In condemning the wisdom of the world, is Paul condemning all wisdom? On what does the deepest wisdom depend?

4

Second Problem:
Incest and the
Community's Indifference (5:1–13)

Within the first two verses of Chapter 5 the reader meets the major elements of a new situation. A man has sinned by living with his father's wife and the community does not seem to have minded it a bit (except for those members who told Paul about this?). But one must note, as a major element of this section of the letter, how Paul takes to curing this twin problem. The man's sexual sin is noted as something "which one would not encounter among pagans"; perhaps Paul is referring to the laws of the pagans which would not allow marriage between a son and his father's wife—if not, Paul is clearly exaggerating, for surely incest within the closest family ties was known throughout the pagan world. Though we do not know the precise situation at this time of Corinth's history, her previous infamy (when she was almost totally destroyed in 146 B.C.) in many matters of morality, sexual included, was notorious; to give an instance, if one intended to search for a prostitute, one was said to "go Corinthing." After the reconstruction of Corinth in 44 B.C., the social and economic circumstances which led to the earlier notoriety repeated themselves—a populace fashioned from people come to work in the transport and allied trades, a workforce streaming in from the variety of the world's cities and bringing with it a maze of ideas and customs—and so one might expect that the same laxness which characterized old Corinth grew anew in this more prosperous city which boasted two ports, which was the gateway between East and West Mediterranean trade and was the capital of an entire Roman province. If Paul was exaggerating when he noted that the

40

Scripture Text

5 It is actually reported that there is immorality among you, and of a kind that is not found even among pagans; for a man is living with his father's wife. [2]And you are arrogant! Ought you not rather to mourn? Let him who has done this be removed from among you.

3 For though absent in body I am present in spirit, and as if present, I have already pronounced judgment [4]in the name of the Lord Jesus on the man who has done such a thing. When you are assembled, and my spirit is present, with the power of our Lord Jesus, [5]you are to deliver this man to Satan for the destruction of the flesh, that his spirit may be saved in the day of the Lord Jesus.

6 Your boasting is not good. Do you not know that a little leaven leavens the whole lump? [7]Cleanse out the old leaven that you may be a new lump, as you really are unleavened. For Christ, our paschal lamb, has been sacrificed. [8]Let us, therefore, celebrate the festival, not with the old leaven, the leaven of malice and evil, but with the unleavened bread of sincerity and truth.

9 I wrote to you in my letter not to associate with immoral men; [10]not at all meaning the immoral of this world, or the greedy and robbers, or idolaters, since then you would need to go out of the world. [11]But rather I wrote to you not to associate with any one who bears the name of brother if he is guilty of immorality or greed, or is an idolater, reviler, drunkard, or robber—not even to eat with such a one. [12]For what have I to do with judging outsiders? Is it not those inside the church whom you are to judge? [13]God judges those outside. "Drive out the wicked person from among you."

Christian was doing something unparalleled among the pagans, he surely was doing this as a way to shake up and impress the Corinthians. Similarly, another example of this major element of these verses is Paul's attack-approach toward the community: the man is wrong, but the community "can be proud of itself"?—it should be in mourning! Thus, not only does Paul present us with the problem of the sinful Christian and with the lax attitude of the community, but he also reveals the approach he has chosen to take, an approach which he no doubt consciously chose to use and which was not simply an unpremeditated outburst of chagrin and anger. It is a concrete situation which he addresses and he must have the prudence to answer it successfully; we see for ourselves the kind of response he has chosen and the language in which he couches it.

Paul's Understanding of the Law of Israel

The law by which God wanted the Israelites to live is spelled out in a number of books of the Old Testament, but particularly in the Book of Leviticus. It is in this foundational book that one reads, among other prohibitions about marriage or sexual relations with one's close relatives: "You must not uncover the nakedness of your father's wife" (Lev 18:8). Though Paul was pre-eminent in recognizing the differences between Christianity and Judaism, he encouraged as valid many of the moral injunctions of the Judaism he had left; he considered them still to be the way God wanted life to be lived. Given his loyalty to the will of God, it is not surprising that he reacts vigorously to disregard for this divine will; and he will react all the more strenuously if the matter is itself serious, if the community considers it a trifling matter and if the entire matter sounds like a return to the paganism the Corinthians had rather recently promised they would turn from, a short-lived hope of a new life slipping back into the lostness of formative years in paganism.

Paul's reaction, then, to this man's sexual practice with "his father's wife" becomes all the more understandable as one realizes what must have been going through the mind of Paul who had labored to

---

JEWISH AND ROMAN LAWS AGAINST INCEST:

Yahweh spoke to Moses:

"Say to the sons of Israel:
'You must not uncover the nakedness of your father's
wife . . . that belongs to your father.' "

Leviticus 18:1-8

"By the Law of the Nations a man commits incest who takes
a wife from among those who closely related to him by
blood."

INSTITUTES, "Digest" Book 23, section 2, number 68
(Mommsen, Theodore. *Corpus Juris Civilis*, Vol. 1, 6th edi-
tion, ed. by Paul Krueger, Berlin, 1954, p. 335.)

---

establish a society which now seemed to have absorbed little and was
far away from him. In response to what he hears from Corinth he
fashions a reply which touches as much the community's attitude as
that of the sinner.

For the sinful man Paul urges excommunication, or so we com-
monly interpret the command to turn him over "to Satan." Given
the history we now know about the uses of excommunication, we
hesitate to approve the notion, particularly when it is found in a foundational document of Christianity. Yet, Paul's expression here shows
that he considers excommunication to be a means to achieve a good:
in this case he hopes that this action will be the means by which the
man can be saved on the day of the Lord. Paul does not spell out the
reasons why he recommends excommunication, but the easy-going
attitude of many Corinthians toward this sin (and the sinner's attitude must be like that of the rest) and the need to impress on the
man and on the community the seriousness of what he has done and
the need to break with those pagan customs which have been so much

a part of their lives for so long—these circumstances surely must have urged Paul to take serious action.

But not only does Paul write an answer which is oriented to discipline of the sinner and those who think like him. He also brings to the mind of all the holiness to which they have been called. They must realize the newness of the life which corresponds to their acceptance of Jesus as Lord; it is in light of this understanding of the reality to which God calls them and to which they have committed themselves that Paul tries to set things straight again.

Excommunication, an attempt to help the individual save himself, is also an attempt to save the community from the infection so easily spread by the sinner. Paul uses the image of the small bit of yeast which affects all the dough it touches, an image which everyone understands. But to this image he adds the meaning implicit in the Jewish practice at Passover of ridding one's entire house of old yeast, so that one has, for the time of the feast, only new bread. This was done, of course, to imitate the Jewish families who left Egypt with unleavened bread, bread that had no yeast. But, besides imitating the bread of that saving time, the Jews also symbolically got rid of the "old" to be replaced by the "new," and Paul is quick to refer "old" and "new" to the "old moral life" and the "new moral life." Thus, the Corinthians are to rid themselves of the old complacence with sin and commit themselves to a new way of life, one untouched by the old elements.

But the thought of Passover and its newness of life cannot but suggest to Paul the reality on which the new life of the Christian is based: the sacrifice of Christ by which the Spirit is bestowed who can give one the strength and guidance actually to live the new life. The Passover, a Jewish feast, is appropriated by the Christians insofar as they can see the lamb of that feast to be Jesus; his death signals the will of God that now, in belief in Jesus, one lives the life God reveals as best for human beings. To get rid of the old yeast of evil and sinfulness, then, is to refuse to make choices in favor of sin. To live the new life as God, the definer of reality, indicates to be the true life for a human being is to live in truth and in honesty; to live otherwise is to deceive oneself and to live in unreality.

An Earlier "First Letter to the Corinthians"

This section of Paul's letter is important because it reveals through Paul's teaching and his disciplining just what role he thinks he should play at this moment in the lives, personal and communal, of this young Corinthian community. But it is also interesting because it unexpectedly gives us the information that Paul had already written a letter to Corinth, at least part of which dealt with the subject of "associating with people of immoral life." The verses which relate this earlier teaching are valuable because they recall to us the somewhat surprising fact that Paul wrote letters which are not included in the New Testament; the process used throughout the early centuries by which the list of New Testament literature came into being does not account, to us today, for the reality of a Pauline letter which never "made it" into the New Testament. The absence of this letter from the final list, however, makes it clear that, should a piece of literature be found in the future which comes from an apostle, it need not be automatically accepted into the New Testament.

But these verses are also interesting because they indicate that the Corinthians were slightly misled by Paul's earlier letter, an indication of intricacies Paul experienced in trying, from a distance, to guide the practices of the Corinthian community. Surely, their misunderstanding of what he wrote is in some part due to the inexperience of the community in the Christian life, an inexperience of judgment which they compensated for by a simplistic reading of Paul's advice. Such a situation has all the earmarks of a young community trying to live a life which is quite new and foreign to it, looking for guidance and not having the experienced judgment to interpret that guidance properly. Such a community it was at Corinth that one can understand better why Paul in this letter before us is so forceful in his presentation of his ideas. He knows how far away he is from the people who need help to live a life to which they are not as yet accustomed, and he knows what price they will have to pay for false guidance or a guidance which is, to them, unclear or muddled. In all this, we understand better how the mind which wrote this letter approached the task.

Moreover, these verses show that the "immorality" of the man who lives with his father's wife, and other types of "immorality," was a subject already treated, certainly by letter and presumably in his teaching at Corinth itself, by a Paul who was anxious to make clearly concrete the implications of one's taking Jesus as one's Lord. Thus, the reaction of Paul, so vigorous in First Corinthians toward the sinner and toward the complacent community, is based on a history of counseling them all precisely against the actions about which he now has to listen.

Association with Sinful Christians

For all Paul's dislike of immorality, he can distinguish clearly the difference between association with non-Christian sinners and association with Christians who are immoral. What is important here is to weigh the effect of associating with a publicly sinful Christian. The Corinthians do not seem to be associating with him out of Christian love which hopes for repentance. Given the dangers inherent in "overlooking" a serious fault, one can only ask oneself, as Paul has asked himself, "How does one bring a new Christian, now a serious sinner, to a renewed life; how does one maintain one's newly acquired sense of life with Jesus, if one associates with a fellow believer who ignores his belief?" Perhaps, all the circumstances considered, one will consider Paul's advice the most prudent. To him, so far away and so aware of the implications of this sinfulness which the community accepts without qualm, a radical measure must be adopted.

The final verse of this section of Paul's letter also gives us a precious insight into the mind of Paul. Though distancing himself from the shape the religion of his forefathers took, Paul still recognized what had been the accepted wisdom handed down in the Hebrew scriptures. In the case of excommunication, Israel had learned, not in theory but in bitter experience, that to associate with those whose lives were based on religious principles opposed to Yahweh was to weaken love of Yahweh and, eventually, to worship another god and follow his ways. Indeed, it was to this "association" that Israel traced those sins for which she was so severely punished by such terrible experiences as hunger, thirst, exile, death. Not speculation, but experience taught them the bitter relationship between association with the disobedient and their own eventual disobedience. Against this background one can appreciate the judgment Paul, so steeped in the wisdom of the Old Testament, passed on to the Corinthians. Perhaps he was overly cautious, overly protective and thus overly harsh in solving an immediate problem, but the long history of Israel is an argument for at least a momentarily severe recommendation. I say "momentarily" because, though the call for excommunication suggests no limits to it, it is quite possible that Paul, in the Second Letter to the Corinthians, is encouraging the community to stop punishment (if not of this man, then certainly of another): "The punishment already imposed by the majority on the man in question is enough; and the best thing now is to give him your forgiveness and encouragement, or he might break down from so much misery. So I am asking you to give some definite proof of your love for him. . . . Anybody you forgive, I forgive . . ." (2 Cor 2:6–10).

Like so many other sections of this letter, 1 Corinthians 5:1–13 is a combination of perennially valid wisdom and wisdom circumscribed by circumstances which can change drastically, as would the judgments created by them, in a very short time.

STUDY QUESTIONS

1. What is the twin problem Paul must now face? What circumstances encouraged the existence of this problem?

2. What possible benefits are there to excommunication? Do you think Paul would have resorted to excommunication if he had been able to go in person to talk with the Corinthians?

3. How are the images of yeast and Passover used by Paul to help his argument?

4. What do we learn from Paul's letter to Corinth which antedates the New Testament's First Letter to the Corinthians?

5. How might we evaluate Paul's urging the Corinthians to separate themselves from sinful Christians?

Third Problem:
Christian Use of Pagan Courts (6:1–11)

As with the case of the man living with his father's wife, so in this case of the use of pagan law courts Paul means to shock his readers by confronting them. This method was chosen probably as the best way to combat laxness or situations in which the Corinthians acted without reference to the commitments implicit in their dedication to Christ and, consequently, to one another. The method Paul uses immediately reminds everyone of a set of criteria from which the actions of the Corinthians are judged and which justify Paul's horror and anger at their ignoring them.

What is assumed or implied in this discussion is the fact that the Corinthians could really have set up their own court. Though what the exact contours and shape of such a court is is not clear, Paul seems to think it realistic to do this. Perhaps he had in mind his experience in Israel where, indeed, there were two full-fledged systems of law and law courts. On the one hand, one had Mosaic law and the Sanhedrin of Jerusalem (as well as local law courts) for the handling of cases in which Mosaic law was involved; on the other hand, one had Roman law and the appropriate courts or tribunals for dealing with cases touching upon Roman law. Sometimes a crime against the one kind of law was equally a crime against the other kind of law, but often the case was not that at all. That is, one might well break the Mosaic law outrageously, without stirring up the slightest interest among Roman judges and vice versa; Jesus is a perfect example of someone who offended the Jewish law most seriously, but who was of no interest to the Roman judges until someone came up

6 When one of you has a grievance against a brother, does he dare go to law before the unrighteous instead of the saints? ²Do you not know that the saints will judge the world? And if the world is to be judged by you, are you incompetent to try trivial cases? ³Do you not know that we are to judge angels? How much more, matters pertaining to this life! ⁴If then you have such cases, why do you lay them before those who are least esteemed by the church? ⁵I say this to your shame. Can it be that there is no man among you wise enough to decide between members of the brotherhood, ⁶but brother goes to law against brother, and that before unbelievers?

7 To have lawsuits at all with one another is defeat for you. Why not rather suffer wrong? Why not rather be defrauded? ⁸But you yourselves wrong and defraud, and that even your own brethren.

9 Do you not know that the unrighteous will not inherit the kingdom of God? Do not be deceived; neither the immoral, nor idolaters, nor adulterers, nor homosexuals, ¹⁰nor thieves, nor the greedy, nor drunkards, nor revilers, nor robbers will inherit the kingdom of God. ¹¹And such were some of you. But you were washed, you were sanctified, you were justified in the name of the Lord Jesus Christ and in the Spirit of our God.

with a crime which broke Roman law. Since the general practice of the conquering Romans was to leave the conquered alone as much as possible, it is most likely that in many places local laws were allowed to flourish and the means to enforce them as well. Thus, Paul is not idealistic when he suggests that the Christians, in some form, act as judges of their own people.

There is a second point to consider in order to understand Paul's approach to the problem of 1 Corinthians 6:1–11; this comes out of Jewish history. To read the history of Israel is to read the history of a people who, though sometimes free and rich (e.g., the time of King Solomon), was often enslaved and impoverished—a people humiliated. Much of the hope or expectation of Israel's happiness was formulated against this suffering and humiliation: Israel looked forward to a time of glory, a time of freedom from its oppressors. Since Israel was the "chosen" one, she pictured herself at times as reaching the state consonant with her "chosenness" if she were placed where the "chosen" should be: at the side of Yahweh. But not only would she be there; she would, with the consent of her beloved Yahweh, exercise with him, or on behalf of him, the office of judge. Particularly was Israel, thus exalted to the right hand of Yahweh, to judge her enemies, to restore the balance of justice which her enemies had overthrown in her enslavement. But, the power to judge was seen to extend really to all peoples, as Yahweh shared his role as universal judge with all his "chosen." Jesus had reminded his Eleven of this imagery when he used it, in an adjusted way, at his Last Supper: "I confer a kingdom on you . . . and you will sit on thrones to judge the twelve tribes of Israel" (Lk 22:30), the Israel who now oppresses Jesus and will soon oppress his disciples. It is not surprising, then, to read in Paul's letter an assumption that the Christians, the "chosen" of God, would be the judges of the entire world, even of angels; Paul is simply extending the old imagery of Israel's writings to depict the reality of the Corinthians' identity, now that they are God's "chosen."

Perhaps it is not surprising any longer to find that such speculative imagery has a history and thus finds its way into Paul's vocabulary. But is it not surprising that Paul chooses to base much of his argument on it? How the Corinthians responded to it is not known, but Paul, true to his fashion in all his correspondence, insists on Christians seeing the fullest significance of their Christianity, even that draped in Jewish imagery of the past, before they begin to act. For proper Christian conduct proceeds best of all from a thorough realization of the connection of action to one's being and dignity: I act this way, because I am this way; I do what I do, because I am what I am.

The Right To Judge Others

Paul's mind moves swiftly, once he begins to line up his arguments against taking fellow Christians to pagan courts. Not only should not the "holy ones" (and Paul always designates his converts as holy)—not only should not the holy ones be judged by the unholy, but the destiny of the holy ones indicates that these are capable and fit to judge in ordinary cases, situations which are far from equal to the judgment to be exercised by the holy ones at the end of the world.

But there is more to this situation than one might at first suspect. Evidently the Corinthians had brought their grievances to their own "judges," only to find them incompetent to judge. Paul, rather than concluding that the only recourse is to go to pagan law courts, presses the community, through shaming them, to put forward men who can be trusted to be reliable judges.

But not only is this a situation in which Christians should be found who can fairly resolve differences among fellow Christians. The very need for a search for judges is to be questioned; that is, why are Christians being brought to trial at all? These who are doing the wrong and cheating should, as implied by their commitment to live the life Jesus led, be willing to be wronged and cheated; yet, so far are they from their calling that they are doing the wronging and the cheating.

Paul recalls to the Corinthians types of people, suggested to him by his own mention of "those who wrong and cheat," who will not inherit the kingdom of God, a description of eternal life carried over from Judaism and a reminder that Paul is now speaking like a prophet of old. The sins of the people mentioned here are clearly understood. That these acts are evil is not simply a revelation given to Christians, but was recognized by the Jewish tradition and in great part by other cultures as well. That they are easily listed suggests that this was not the first time that such sins were organized in list-form, nor the first time that the Corinthians had heard them described in list-form; both the sins and their listing were no doubt part of the endless teaching in which Paul tried to make clear over eighteen months in Corinth the implications of life with Jesus, accepted through the formal commitment of baptism.

Baptism Leads to Justification

Indeed, Paul has turned his attention once again, as he ends this section, to the reality of what a Christian is, with the implication that from such a reality should flow only certain kinds of conduct. The description he uses is his but belongs as well to the tradition of early Christianity. Baptism has as one of its meanings "to wash," as the water flows over the immersed neophyte and the sacrament cleanses from the uncleanness of sin. This "cleansing" is the kind that will let the Christian stand in the presence of God rather than be banished from it because one is unworthy because of past deeds; the Christian, in other words, is made holy, able to stand in the presence of Holiness. But the washing away of sin can also be translated into another Pauline image, drawn from the experience of law courts. That is, one is to transfer to God the action of a judge who declares innocent or just a person who knows he is guilty and whom the judge knows to be guilty. This "making the unjust just" is the effect of Jesus' offering himself on behalf of the unjust, precisely so that the effect of justification (the "making someone just") may happen. The term which sums up this justification due to Jesus' total self-giving is "baptism in the name of the Lord Jesus Christ." By baptism one acknowledges Jesus' irreplaceable role in God's will to justify one who cannot earn justification; by it one also commits oneself to live a life different from that which caused one's lack of justice. It is noteworthy that the baptism is in the name of "the Lord Jesus Christ"; the titles "Lord" and "Christ" are succinct summaries of the Christian's belief about Jesus, professions of commitment to him and thus very fitting for the rite of baptism itself.

But, when it comes to baptism, Paul must refer not only to the name of Jesus, but to the Spirit of God as well. For with baptism comes the outpouring of the Spirit, the sharing by God of an essential element of his being. It was common enough in the first century to think of a human being as composed of three essential elements: body, soul and spirit. Forced to think of God in human terms and aware of the "Spirit of Yahweh" in the Jewish scriptures, Paul sees in God the essential element of Spirit, a Spirit of holiness, a Spirit of all that God is. To the extent that it is possible, God at baptism shares his Spirit, thus offering to the believer the most intimate relationship, the sharing of his Self, the greatest gift of his love.

A final observation concerning this section of Paul's letter is this, that one must always remember the distinction between objective and subjective guilt when dealing with condemnations such as Paul gives here in connection with his list of those "who will not inherit the kingdom of God." That is, though it is reasonable to show the incompatibility of certain kinds of sins and the kingdom of God (again the Jewish phrase), it is impossible to know the degree of guilt a person incurs by performing one of these sins. Not only is this a rule in religious matters; it pervades all reasonable legal systems.

In a sense, Paul has lessened his interest in the problem of Christians going to law courts; rather, he has come to concentrate his final words on the cause of the litigations, the Christian's offensive actions. Paul wants the immediate problem regarding the use of pagan courts solved, but he is finally concerned with the love of Christian for Christian, the perseverance to reach the kingdom of God, and the harmony of the community which is rooted in love and justice.

Study Questions

1. Why does it seem likely that the Christians could have set up their own law courts?

2. What is the Old Testament history of the image of judgment, by which Christians can be described as "judges of the world"?

3. Why should Christians not take other Christians to pagan courts?

4. What is a major source of morality for Paul? Explain.

5. Explain cleansing, justification, the meaning of "the Spirit."

6. What is the difference between objective guilt and subjective guilt? How is this distinction to be used in relation to Paul's list of sins?

6

Fourth Problem: Immoral Sexual Liaisons (6:12–20)

Paul must, a second time, address a problem regarding the misuse of sexual action; whereas earlier he dealt with a man who was living with his father's wife, he now takes up the problem of fornication. One must again recall the circumstances which we think existed in Corinth at this time, particularly the general apathy or indifference to most any sexual activity and the difficulty of changing one's attitudes and actions after living with and by them for so many years; indeed, while a person like Paul was present to lead, there might be calm, but, once the persuasive leader is gone, reversion to old habits is very possible.

A second and particular factor which added to the laxity of Corinth toward expressions of a sexual nature was the involvement of sexual intercourse in pagan worship rites. For a long, long time human beings, in search of some way to reach immortality, saw in sexual intercourse at least a moment in which one actually shared in the creation of life; for a moment one was a god. In its own way this insight was dignified, for the mystery of life-giving is essentially enveloped in the act of intercourse. But as far as Judaism and Christianity were concerned, paganism had, at its best, encouraged a misuse of intercourse, by urging believers to engage in sexual intercourse with prostitutes officially designated for this purpose—and had made possible eventual misuse of sex on a grand scale. Pagan converts to Christianity often were asked to stop practices which not only society in general accepted, but even the authority of religion encouraged.

Let us enter into the manner in which Paul addresses this prob-

SCRIPTURE TEXT

12 "All things are lawful for me," but not all things are helpful. "All things are lawful for me," but I will not be enslaved by anything. [13]"Food is meant for the stomach and the stomach for food"—and God will destroy both one and the other. The body is not meant for immorality, but for the Lord, and the Lord for the body. [14]And God raised the Lord and will also raise us up by his power. [15]Do you not know that your bodies are members of Christ? Shall I therefore take the members of Christ and make them members of a prostitute? Never! [16]Do you not know that he who joins himself to a prostitute becomes one body with her? For, as it is written, "The two shall become one." [17]But he who is united to the Lord becomes one spirit with him. [18]Shun immorality. Every other sin which a man commits is outside the body; but the immoral man sins against his own body. [19]Do you not know that your body is a temple of the Holy Spirit within you, which you have from God? You are not your own; [20]you were bought with a price. So glorify God in your body.

lem of fornication. Paul does not immediately mention "fornication," but prefers to deal with the principle by which people are justifying fornication. The principle at stake is this, that "everything is permitted to me." Is this principle in some way a misunderstanding of the freedom Paul talked about in speaking of the Christian as free from the Mosaic law? Or is it the result of influence of pagan thinking? Or is Paul simply making a guess, even a shrewd one, as to the reason why some Christians think they can commit fornication? We are not sure as to the source of this principle, but it is clearly the grounding, Paul thinks, of the fornication reported to him, and he enters the problem through this principle.

Paul's answers to this principle are brief; he presumes that the principle, "everything is permitted to me," can be understood to be a legitimate one, but can be accepted more fully only when it is considered in the light of two observations Paul makes.

First, many situations in life show that, though one "theoretically" can do something, one's own good strongly suggests that one not do it. Thus, nature itself argues that "freedom" is subordinated to and limited by a higher principle: what is for one's good. Second, many times what one calls a choice made in freedom is not that at all, but is rather a choice made because one is subtly enslaved to the thing chosen, often without being aware of it; what appears to be freely chosen is really a thing over which I have no choice.

The application of these observations are clear in the case of fornication: Paul will not contradict one's claim to self-determination and choice, but he will ask if a person is choosing what is best for himself (what is for his good), and he will ask the person to decide if he is choosing fornication out of freedom or out of enslavement to sex. It is, of course, Paul's conviction that people can often deceive themselves in claiming indifference to sexual action and his conviction that every choice in favor of sexual action is not automatically for the good of the total person. Paul argues for freedom, but for a freedom which serves one's total well-being, for a freedom is which true freedom.

Paul next takes up an argument based on parallelism in nature.

PROSTITUTION IN CORINTH

"It is an ancient custom in Corinth . . . whenever the city prays to Aphrodite (Goddess of Love) in matters of grave importance, to invite as many prostitutes as possible to join in their petitions and later these women add their supplications to the goddess and are present at the sacrifices."

"Corinth celebrated a festival in honor of Aphrodite for the prostitutes. . . . On these days it is customary for the prostitutes to revel, and it is quite in the mode for them to get drunk here in our company."

Athenaeus, (*Deipnosophistae*)
(Murphy-O'Connor, O.P., Jerome. *St. Paul's Corinth*, Good News Studies 6, Glazier, Delaware, 1983, pp. 126–127.)

It is clear that food and stomach relate to each other by nature—a morally just relationship, for nature dictates it. One should be able to draw the parallel: the body is made for sexual relations, and sexual relations are expected of the body. Paul has to draw some distinction between the first pair (food–stomach) and the second pair (body–sexual relations). He does it by recalling the resurrection from the dead, which teaches that, though the person rises with a body, he does not rise with the needs of this world he leaves behind, specifically with the need for sexual relations. No, food, stomach, and sexuality that is associated with preservation and continuance of life in this world will not be part of the new age; the body will be a glorified body.

Having established a distinction between body, on the one hand, and food-stomach, on the other, Paul drives home the point of the distinction: what will rise, what will accompany the human being into the next age is not simply ruled by the laws of this world, but is ruled by the One who will raise the Christian from the dead.

The body belongs to its Lord, by the free choice made public in baptism; it is the body God will somehow reproduce as the glorified body of the risen Christian.

Paul has reached his central argument against fornication. His mention of the Lord, of one's Master, leads him to recall the intimate relationship established by baptism between Jesus and the believer. One is not only united with the will of Jesus (which shuns fornication), but one is also a member of Christ. For Paul, Christ has a body which is not to be confused with his personal body in which he lives risen forever. No, this "other" body of Christ is made up of Christians who are all its members, so intimate is the union produced at baptism. At baptism they become alive with Christ's Spirit; thus, they are like limbs which live by the life of a person. Since this life is real, the in-living is real; Christ has a body of members joined to him by love and part of him because it is his life which enlivens them.

True Understanding of Baptismal Vows

Reminding the Corinthians of their very intimate relationship with Jesus, a relationship of obedience and a relationship of shared life of God, Paul can reasonably ask the Corinthians how they can justify their giving themselves to another person by a giving that clearly ruptures the union they had already given themselves to in baptism. Fornication is a contradiction of an intimacy already agreed to.

Paul also reminds the Corinthians that fornication (which now switches to prostitution) is a real uniting of two people; there is no getting away from the degree of unity natural to intercourse. The commitment is complete, and the rupture with Christ is equally complete. It is the same sexual act which the Old Testament has in mind when it speaks of two becoming one; it is oneness with Christ, formed in baptism, which is now abandoned for oneness with a prostitute.

Paul, in citing the Old Testament, uses the clause: the two become one flesh. Anxious not to be misunderstood, he adjusts this clause to the reality of oneness with Christ; one had the deepest intimacy with him, but it is a union through the sharing of the Holy Spirit, not through the sharing of flesh.

Another argument Paul raises against fornication is an argument intended to show the seriousness of the sin. All other sins are committed outside the body; this is the only one committed against the body. One might be able to come up with a sin against one's own self besides fornication, but Paul has substantially made his point about the "suicidal" nature of fornication; one destroys oneself with this sin.

Paul concludes with two arguments drawn from the fullness of Christian reality. First, one has dwelling in oneself the Holy Spirit of God; one is by definition a temple. To sin against a temple is the more tragic, for one thereby commits a sin against a most sacred place, the very home of God. Second, one has been bought back by God, and the price was the blood of Jesus. No matter what may be one's sense of independence, one is really, because of this buying back, the possession of God. One's happiness results from it. To sell oneself to another is to lose all that had been gained by Christ and given in baptism. One gives up the very goal to which his freedom should lead him.

One should note explicitly that Paul's major argument against fornication/prostitution is not based on the incompatibility of sexual relations and membership in the body of Christ; otherwise, marriage would be denied Christians. Paul's argument is meaningful only where the sexual relationship is already known to be wrong because it is against God's will.

STUDY QUESTIONS

1. What was the general, public climate or attitude in Corinth toward fornication/prostitution?

2. How does Paul deal with the principle, "Everything is permitted to me"? Does he answer this principle well?

3. Why is it not permissible in logic to argue from "food for stomach, therefore body for sex"? That is, in the light of belief in Jesus, how is "body" different from "food, sex, stomach"?

4. Why does fornication/prostitution contradict a Christian's baptism?

5. How influential in today's society do you think Paul's arguments can be against intercourse outside marriage?

Fifth Problem: Proper Understanding of Celibacy and Marriage (7:1–40)

For a third (and last) time, Paul takes up questions having to do with sexual relationships; having dealt with a specific case of incest and with probably more than one case of fornication/prostitution, Paul takes up the more general question of legitimate marriage and its sexual component. The source from which Paul learns about the marriage practice in the Corinthian community is not that from which he has learned about the incest and fornication carried on by some community members: the former comes from a letter (or letters) written to Paul and dealing with the problems which run to the end of Paul's First Letter to the Corinthians; the latter comes from a verbal report to Paul by "Chloe's people" (1:11).

The primary statement of Chapter 7, to which all the thoughts of Paul in this chapter are somehow related, is to be found in the very first verse: "It is a good thing that a man not touch a woman." By "touch" Paul is usually understood to mean "marry," with concern for sexual relations in marriage. How might one explain the problem to which this statement of Paul is the answer? There is no common suggestion given by interpreters; indeed, a degree of speculation must be allowed for lack of much clear evidence.

It seems to me likely, in view of the fact that the Corinthians have written to Paul on the subject of sexual relations in marriage (7:1), that Paul, in his earlier teaching in Corinth, had in some way praised and even encouraged a life of celibacy in pursuit of the love of Christ. His own life was a tribute to the union of spirituality and

7 Now concerning the matters about which you wrote. It is well for a man not to touch a woman. ²But because of the temptation to immorality, each man should have his own wife and each woman her own husband. ³The husband should give to his wife her conjugal rights, and likewise the wife to her husband. ⁴For the wife does not rule over her own body, but the husband does; likewise the husband does not rule over his own body, but the wife does. ⁵Do not refuse one another except perhaps by agreement for a season, that you may devote yourselves to prayer; but then come together again, lest Satan tempt you through lack of self-control. ⁶I say this by way of concession, not of command. ⁷I wish that all were as I myself am. But each has his own special gift fom God, one of one kind and one of another.

8 To the unmarried and the widows I say that it is well for them to remain single as I do. ⁹But if they cannot exercise self-control, they should marry. For it is better to marry than to be aflame with passion.

10 To the married I give charge, not I but the Lord, that the wife should not separate from the husband ¹¹(but if she does, let her remain single or else be reconciled to her husband)—and that the husband should not divorce his wife.

12 To the rest I say, not the Lord, that if any brother has a wife who is an unbeliever, and she consents to live with him, he should not divorce her. ¹³If any woman has a husband who is an unbeliever, and he consents to live with her, she should not divorce him. ¹⁴For the unbelieving husband is consecrated through his wife, and the unbelieving wife is consecrated through her husband. Otherwise, your children would be un-

clean, but as it is they are holy. [15]But if the unbelieving partner desires to separate, let it be so; in such a case the brother or sister is not bound. For God has called us to peace. [16]Wife, how do you know whether you will save your husband? Husband, how do you know whether you will save your wife?

17 Only, let every one lead the life which the Lord has assigned to him, and in which God has called him. This is my rule in all the churches. [18]Was any one at the time of his call already circumcised? Let him not seek to remove the marks of circumcision. Was any one at the time of his call uncircumcised? Let him not seek circumcision. [19]For neither circumcision counts for anything nor uncircumcision, but keeping the commandments of God. [20]Every one should remain in the state in which he was called. [21]Were you a slave when called? Never mind. But if you can gain your freedom, avail yourself of the opportunity. [22]For he who was called in the Lord as a slave is a freedman of the Lord. Likewise he who was free when called is a slave of Christ. [23]You were bought with a price; do not become slaves of men. [24]So, brethren, in whatever state each was called, there let him remain with God.

25 Now concerning the unmarried, I have no command of the Lord, but I give my opinion as one who by the Lord's mercy is trustworthy. [26]I think that in view of the impending distress it is well for a person to remain as he is. [27]Are you bound to a wife? Do not seek to be free. Are you free from a wife? Do not seek marriage. [28]But if you marry, you do not sin, and if a girl marries she does not sin. Yet those who marry will have worldly troubles, and I would spare you that. [29]I mean, brethren, the appointed time has grown very short; from now on, let those who have wives live as though they had none, [30]and those who mourn as though they were not mourning, and those who rejoice as though they were not rejoicing, and those who buy as though they had no goods, [31]and those who deal

with the world as though they had no dealings with it. For the form of this world is passing away.

32 I want you to be free from anxieties. The unmarried man is anxious about the affairs of the Lord, how to please the Lord; [33]but the married man is anxious about worldly affairs, how to please his wife, [34]and his interests are divided. And the unmarried woman or girl is anxious about the affairs of the Lord, how to be holy in body and spirit; but the married woman is anxious about worldly affairs, how to please her husband. [35]I say this for your own benefit, not to lay any restraint upon you, but to promote good order and to secure your undivided devotion to the Lord.

36 If any one thinks that he is not behaving properly toward his betrothed, if his passions are strong, and it has to be, let him do as he wishes: let them marry—it is no sin. [37]But whoever is firmly established in his heart, being under no necessity but having his desire under control, and has determined this in his heart, to keep her as his betrothed, he will do well. [38]So that he who marries his betrothed does well; and he who refrains from marriage will do better.

39 A wife is bound to her husband as long as he lives. If the husband dies, she is free to be married to whom she wishes, only in the Lord. [40]But in my judgment she is happier if she remains as she is. And I think that I have the Spirit of God.

celibacy; indeed, it was natural enough for Paul to see his celibacy as a means by which to achieve the psychological single-mindedness he found so valuable in relating to Christ. The newly-converted Corinthians, concomitantly, were enthusiastic and idealistic enough to try to follow both the words and life of Paul; in this first fervor of dedication, they, reacting against the excessive sexuality of Corinth and quite the contrary of those other Christians who committed sexual sins of incest and fornication (or easily tolerated them), anxiously considered giving up a sexual life without much thought as to the prudence of such a decision.

Paul, now, is faced with questions about the wisdom of total abstinence from sexual life, an abstinence which, I believe, he somehow has inculcated in some of his converts. The easiest reply Paul could have mailed back would be the advice to forget his own way of life and his praise of celibacy; he would do this on the grounds that it would simply be the most direct way to eliminate the quandary over "marriage or no marriage," "sex within marriage or no sex within marriage."

But Paul is convinced of certain things and will prefer to deal with the complications they may create, rather than simplify problems by muting his own convictions. Thus, what we find in Chapter 7 is a careful balancing of two values, that of celibacy and that of marriage (or sex within marriage). Put more exactly, what we have here is not a chapter treating the values of marriage or licit sex (perhaps Ephesians 5:21–33 does this best?), but an effort to maintain the value of celibacy while affirming the goodness and sure value of marriage.

Even before dealing with the individual situations Paul treats in this chapter, one should be aware of two factors which color all of Paul's thoughts here; each is visible in the chapter. First, the ultimate advice of Paul to any individual Christian considering this matter of marriage and celibacy is drawn from verse 7. While restating his preference for celibacy, Paul has the deeper insight that both marriage and celibacy are gifts from God, and that each person has his/her own particular gift from him. Thus, marriage is a gift, as is celibacy; and one must discover one's gift and, it is hoped, accept it.

No matter what one argues in regard to the value of these matters on the level of abstraction from concrete circumstances, one must eventually ask the questions which deal with the individual, unique person: what is *my* gift? Paul clearly believes, therefore, that marriage is no situation into which one falls because one cannot be celibate; marriage is a gift. To think of it in any other way is to miss a most significant point. Thus, Paul believes that, no matter what the arguments pro and con about marriage/celibacy on the theoretical level, the decisive question rests on the practical level, where one must make a prudential judgment as to one's own personal gift from God.

Second, as seen in various parts of the chapter most explicitly, Paul does not back down from his personal conviction about the greater potential for psychological union with Christ coming from the state of celibacy. One might argue that Paul's own celibacy is a hindrance to his appreciation of marriage; there is no doubt, however, that he alerts Christians to the value of celibacy which otherwise might not be seriously appreciated and considered as a way to Christ. With these two thoughts in mind, then, let us look carefully at Paul's advice to the Corinthians on this matter about which they wrote to him, their "founding and spiritual father."

The Marital Relationship

The advice, "it is a good thing for a man not to touch a woman," is first applied to the situation of a married couple. Evidently various marriage partners wanted to respond to the "suggestion of celibacy" by prolonged sexual abstinence, if divorce was impossible. Paul's response has a number of remarkable points to it. First, though Paul never encourages a person to marry this or that person simply because one wants sexual relations, he is well aware that the drive of sex is to be answered by marriage, the situation in which each person has his or her own wife or husband. Second, he knows, though he himself is celibate, that the love involved in marriage is so generous that, in

EXCERPTS FROM ROMAN MARRIAGE LAWS:

"Marriage is the union of male and female and the sharing of
all aspects of life; marriage is acknowledged by both divine and
human law."

number 1

"Marriage cannot take place unless all are in agreement, i.e.,
both those who are entering it and those in whose power the
marriage partners might be."

number 2

INSTITUTES "Digest" Book 23 section 2 (Mommsen, Theodore. *Corpus Juris Civilis,* Vol. 1, 6th ed, ed. by Paul Krueger, Berlin, 1954, p. 330.)

"Marriage is nullified by divorce, death, captivity or other
chance servitude of either married partner."

INSTITUTES "Digest" Book 24 section 2 number 1 (*Idem,* p.
355.)

it, one gives one's body to one's partner; so generous is the lover that
he or she grants to the beloved a right to physical union. Third, Paul
is aware, perhaps because of his celibacy, that union with God can
be helped by turning the psyche away from physical satisfaction or
pleasure; even so, he is equally aware of the prudence needed to know
when to abstain from sexual intercourse and very much aware that
both partners to this intense union of marriage must freely agree to
this abstention—the existing marriage clearly takes precedence over
a desire for God through sexual abstinence. Paul, then, hardly coun-
sels celibacy in any form for those already married unless optimum
conditions allow for some sexual abstinence, conditions, that is,

which do not threaten in any way the unitive love of marriage. Indeed, Paul's emphasis on giving one's body to one's partner has become a hallmark by which is expressed the profundity of marital vows.

Widows and the Unmarried

Paul's second response is advice to "widows and the unmarried"; to these he suggests his preference of a celibate life, but again with realism regarding the sexual drive and its satisfaction. If it be a drive which is strong enough, a Christian should not answer it with an imprudence based on a misunderstanding of Paul's praise of celibacy. One's sexual makeup may well suggest marriage; again, however, Paul understands this as an indication for marriage, not as the reason why one marries this person rather than that. Sex suggests marriage; love determines whom one marries and when.

The Question of Divorce

In dealing with the question of celibacy for people already married, Paul clearly refuses (vv 10–16) to think of celibacy demanding divorce; such an idea as divorce was far from his mind when he spoke highly of celibacy. What is of great interest in his reasoning here is his reference to what is "from the Lord," namely that one does not leave one's husband or wife, or, if that happens, that one either make up with the partner or remain unmarried. Paul is here opening to our eyes one strand of the great tradition of teaching coming to him (and to others) "from the Lord." Paul, though an interpreter of God's will for his churches, is very much aware of his dependence on the tradition which precedes and informs him. The uniformity of teaching which we receive through the Lucan, Marcan and Pauline writings, that Jesus taught that marriage does not allow for divorce, suggests that the words of Jesus in the Matthean tradition, wherein divorce seems to be allowed for a defined sexual misbehavior, is an adjustment to Jesus' own teaching. And Paul, having cited the authority of Jesus in this matter of divorce, will now create another exception to Jesus' words.

An Exception to the Rule Against Divorce

Paul is deliberately clear in distinguishing between Jesus' teaching about divorce and the judgment he himself is to offer the Corinthians regarding a particular circumstance of a marriage. It seems reasonable to conclude from Paul's words that one partner of an already existing marriage has converted to belief in Christ and that this new religious commitment has in various ways so disturbed the non-Christian partner that the latter chooses to end the marriage. Given the will of the non-Christian partner and aware of what might happen to the Christian partner if Paul forces the marriage to continue out of an obedience which is given to a religion in which the non-believer does not believe—given all this, Paul accepts the divorce of the two partners as legitimate. Paul will not allow the marriage bond to be broken by the choice of the Christian; the decision to divorce must come from the non-believing partner.

Paul suggests two reasons why the Christian should remain faithful, as long as the non-believer is content with the marriage. First, though he never explains this further and though no religious group based on the New Testament has ever taught this, Paul indicates that the non-Christian partner is made "one with the saints" by virtue of union with the Christian partner; the proof of this "oneness with the saints" is the holiness of the children (not said to result from baptism), a holiness which would be impossible if one of the parents was unholy. One can understand the logic Paul uses, but no one has ever explained the nature of this "oneness with the saints" that seemingly automatically made "clean," just by being children of a believer. Second, as long as the marriage lasts, there is always hope that through it the non-Christian partner will be saved by the

Christian partner; Paul is probably suggesting that the believer may
lead the non-believer to faith in Jesus.

Thus, Paul is quite conservative in his permission for divorce,
and is far, far from allowing divorce for the reason with which this
entire discussion began: that "it is good for a man not to touch a
woman." Paul's major concern in allowing divorce at all was the
"peace" of the Christian partner (and the faith, as well), which would
be destroyed by an unbeliever who wants to destroy the marriage.
This situation is far from that with which the chapter began, for in
Paul's thinking marriage between two believers has the potential for
bringing great peace and strong faith, not for destroying peace.

Considerations in Marital Decision-Making

Having spoken to the married, the unmarried and the widowed
regarding the value of celibacy for them, Paul adds a principle for
decision-making which he notes he has given to all the churches; it
is intended for the peace of so many who, already adults, had become
believers. Like the Corinthians in their anxious questions about
changing their states of life to embrace celibacy as a demand of their
newly accepted religion, many converts to Christ felt this same pull
to abandon the situations in which they were when converted to reach
some other state which appeared to be demanded by their belief in
Christ. Somehow, through the official preachers or by other means,
clarity as to what was really necessary for salvation often became ob-
scured. Celibacy, changing the marks of circumcision, freedom from
slavery—somehow one was thought to lose the opportunity for salvation if one did not do these, or other things. The question here is
not the value of celibacy or of freedom from slavery; the question is
whether, if one cannot be celibate or freed, one can be saved or not.
Paul's advice, then, to stay as you were is not meant to limit one's
freedom; it is meant to calm the anxiety of those who confuse their
state of life with what is necessary for salvation. Paul suggests what
the true necessity really is when speaking of freedom and slavery: he

advises the Christian to "be the slave of no one." In this he means that one be a slave only of one Lord, Jesus, who, after the manner of a lord, bought his slave—and with his own blood. Obviously, such slavery is concerned with devotion and fidelity to the Lord's will, which is necessary for salvation; one is not to follow the will of others as though they determined the way to salvation. Yet, does not Paul unwittingly write the words which cause again the confusion of the past? By saying "Do not become slaves of men" (v 23), is he not opening himself to the interpretation that one must seek physical freedom, impossible though it might seem in this first-century society, in order to be saved?

Paul's mind turns again to the specific question put to him concerning celibacy. To be fair, he clearly states that Jesus gave no directions about the need for his followers to be celibate, but Paul cannot deny the value he has found in remaining faithful in a celibate life. Paul is now thinking of those who are virgins and he draws from his own experience the conclusion that it "is good for a man not to touch a woman." He repeats, too, that this valued celibacy need not make a person change a state of life and again affirms that to marry is not to be considered a sin.

But there surface at this point factors which Paul sees can make marriage less desirable. First, Paul has come to know the troubles that can be a significant part of marriage; he wants to spare the unmarried such troubles. Second, Paul looks at marriage, indeed all of the institutions that belong to the preservation and development of this age only, against the reality of the shortness of this age. Third, marriage does not afford the same degree of psychologically aware union between Christ and the Christian as does celibacy; in order to make a marriage successful, one must attend to many other things than Christ.

Aspects of the New Age

The first and third considerations are clear enough and can be tested by any reader with the requisite experience. The middle or second Pauline idea, however, needs some comment. One of the ways in which the Old Testament envisions the future is to distinguish between "our" age or eon which we experience in all its "this-world-liness" and the age or eon which will replace it and be the time of perfection. The replacement of one age by another is God's work, and may be signaled by God's sending someone, anointed for the task, to begin the new age; this person, the Anointed One (= Messiah or Christ), is identified by the Christians as Jesus. For Paul, aspects of the new age have been introduced into this age, even though it has not altogether passed into the new age; it was the death and resurrection of Christ which shares with the believer death to sin and its ally, death, and the principle of life by which one lives in the new age, the Spirit of God. Thus, one has already in some ways begun to live the eternal life with God which characterizes the new age, having overcome the most characteristic qualities of this age: sin and the death which keeps one dead. With these gifts received by which the new age is introduced into this age, Paul can see only too clearly the passing of this age, its total ending; he expects it soon. For anyone who has experienced the awareness that old, conventional things are passing into something new, where the past will no longer be the reality—for such a person, it is understandable how Paul can suggest that one concentrate on the new world and not be caught as one simply embroiled or engrossed in the world that now passes. It is Paul's contention that celibacy offers a person more opportunity to concentrate one's forces on the reality of this imminent new age than does marriage, or any other human institution of this age which exacts one's energies for the preservation and development of this age only.

There is no doubt that there is wisdom, great wisdom, in Paul's experience of union with the Lord through celibacy. But given his awareness that marriage is a gift from God and his conviction that marriage is a valid way to live one's commitment to the Lord, he no doubt could have written at length about how marital love can bring one successfully into the new age, and he would approve our efforts to make this clear. Here, however, he is more intent on walking the thin line between praising celibacy and demanding it as the only response compatible with faith in Christ.

Two Final Points

In closing our comments on this Chapter 7, I should draw attention to two points. First, verses 36–38 are so written in the original Greek that Paul could be understood to be speaking of a case in which a man must decide (as was the custom in those days) as to whether or not to marry off his daughter or of a case of two engaged people who must decide whether or not to go through with their marriage. The Greek offers this option because it is not perfectly clear; translations, however, must make a choice, and so one will find these verses translated one way one time, another way another time, either about a man and his daughter, or about an engaged couple.

Second, the chapter ends with a frank admission that Paul's preference for celibacy is his opinion. He claims, without irony I believe, that his judgment is guided by the Spirit of God; even so, his preference is still referred to as an opinion, and he quite honestly admits that those who disagree with him might have the Spirit of God, too. Paul presses his opinion hard, but always fairly, without unjust exaggeration, and with respect for the judgment of others. He presses harder than might seem necessary, for he is "the father of the community" which needs his guidance so badly; their appeal to him to help solve their problems shows this very clearly.

With the completion of Chapter 7, we have seen all that Paul will say in regard to the problems involving sexuality in the Corinthian community. What a variety of aspirations and attitudes must have characterized this small community of Christians, which on the one hand knew a case of incest and seemingly accepted it as well as cases of fornication or prostitution, and on the other hand was anxious about living a life of celibacy, even to the point of being willing to break up a marriage! It falls to Paul to give prudent advice to all— and to do it by letter and from hundreds of miles away! Since there were many views about sexuality lived out in the robust port city of Corinth, views ranging from unrestrained freedom to severe asceticism, Paul had his hands full in trying to instruct converts of three years or less in these delicate matters.

Study Questions

1. Why has "celibacy" become a problem in the Corinthian Church and who is affected by this problem?

2. What is the meaning of verse 7 and what role does it play in Paul's advice in Chapter 7?

3. Evaluate Paul's advice to Christians who are married but want to practice prolonged celibacy.

4. How does Paul approach divorce. Is it allowed in order to practice celibacy? Is it allowed for any reason? Is Paul's advice in accord with Jesus' teaching?

5. Is freedom from slavery necessary for salvation?

6. In what ways might celibacy be considered a better state of life than marriage?

7. Explain the Old Testament background of the terms "this age" and "the age to come"; relate them to marriage/celibacy.

Sixth Problem:
Idol Worship (8:1–11:1)

It is helpful to realize that Chapters 8, 9 and 10 form one literary unity. The formal unifying subject grounding Paul's remarks is the "eating of meat offered to idols." More concretely, the subject is divisible into two very unequal parts, the longer dealing with "eating meat which *has been* offered to idols," the shorter dealing with "eating meat which *is being* offered to idols." Everything in these three chapters, then, is somehow logically related to the eating of meat which has been or is being offered to idols.

As elsewhere, so in Corinth, where the tiny Christian community lived amid pagans and often shared experiences as neighbors will do, the reality of pagan worship was part of everyone's daily consciousness. This reality presented two problems, each of which has been solved erroneously; often uncharitableness has accompanied the false solutions in the Corinthian community. What exactly occurred in Corinth, insofar as we can discern it?

First, let us look at how the first part of the problem arose, that of "eating meat which *has been* offered to idols." There were sacrifices in abundance offered each week at the major shrines in the Corinthian city. A good part of these sacrifices involved the flesh of animals. Despite the type of sacrifice known as holocaust, in which the entire offering of meat was totally burned, there was a great deal of meat which was offered, even somewhat burned or boiled, and then equivalently "left over," for clearly the gods to whom the offerings were made did not eat it. True, the priests often were the recipients of the meat left over from the sacrifices, and often the rules of some sacri-

8 Now concerning food offered to idols: we know that "all of us possess knowledge." "Knowledge" puffs up, but love builds up. [2]If any one imagines that he knows something, he does not yet know as he ought to know. [3]But if one loves God, one is known by him.

4 Hence, as to the eating of food offered to idols, we know that "an idol has no real existence," and that "there is no God but one." [5]For although there may be so-called gods in heaven or on earth—as indeed there are many "gods" and many "lords"—[6]yet for us there is one God, the Father, from whom are all things and for whom we exist, and one Lord, Jesus Christ, through whom are all things and through whom we exist.

7 However, not all possess this knowledge. But some, through being hitherto accustomed to idols, eat food as really offered to an idol; and their conscience, being weak, is defiled. [8]Food will not commend us to God. We are no worse off if we do not eat, and no better off if we do. [9]Only take care lest this liberty of yours somehow become a stumbling block to the weak. [10]For if any one sees you, a man of knowledge, at table in an idol's temple, might he not be encouraged, if his conscience is weak, to eat food offered to idols? [11]And so by your knowledge this weak man is destroyed, the brother for whom Christ died. [12]Thus, sinning against your brethren and wounding their conscience when it is weak, you sin against Christ. [13]Therefore, if food is a cause of my brother's falling, I will never eat meat, lest I cause my brother to fall.

9 Am I not free? Am I not an apostle? Have I not seen Jesus our Lord? Are not you my workmanship in the Lord? [2]If

to others I am not an apostle, at least I am to you; for you are the seal of my apostleship in the Lord.

3 This is my defense to those who would examine me. [4]Do we not have the right to our food and drink? [5]Do we not have the right to be accompanied by a wife, as the other apostles and the brothers of the Lord and Cephas? [6]Or is it only Barnabas and I who have no right to refrain from working for a living? [7]Who serves as a soldier at his own expense? Who plants a vineyard without eating any of its fruit? Who tends a flock without getting some of the milk?

8 Do I say this on human authority? Does not the law say the same? [9]For it is written in the law of Moses, "You shall not muzzle an ox when it is treading out the grain." Is it for oxen that God is concerned? [10]Does he not speak entirely for our sake? It was written for our sake, because the plowman should plow in hope and the thresher thresh in hope of a share in the crop. [11]If we have sown spiritual good among you, is it too much if we reap your material benefits? [12]If others share this rightful claim upon you, do not we still more?

Nevertheless, we have not made use of this right, but we endure anything rather than put an obstacle in the way of the gospel of Christ. [13]Do you not know that those who are employed in the temple service get their food from the temple, and those who serve at the altar share in the sacrificial offerings? [14]In the same way, the Lord commanded that those who proclaim the gospel should get their living by the gospel.

15 But I have made no use of any of these rights, nor am I writing this to secure any such provision. For I would rather die than have any one deprive me of my ground for boasting. [16]For if I preach the gospel, that gives me no ground for boasting. For necessity is laid upon me. Woe to me if I do not preach the gospel! [17]For if I do this of my own will, I have a reward; but if not of my own will, I am entrusted with a commission. [18]What then is my reward? Just this: that in my preaching I

may make the gospel free of charge, not making full use of my right in the gospel.

19 For though I am free from all men, I have made myself a slave to all, that I might win the more. [20]To the Jews I became as a Jew, in order to win Jews; to those under the law I became as one under the law—though not being myself under the law—that I might win those under the law. [21]To those outside the law I became as one outside the law—not being without law toward God but under the law of Christ—that I might win those outside the law. [22]To the weak I became weak, that I might win the weak. I have become all things to all men, that I might by all means save some. [23]I do it all for the sake of the gospel, that I may share in its blessings.

24 Do you not know that in a race all the runners compete, but only one receives the prize? So run that you may obtain it. [25]Every athlete exercises self-control in all things. They do it to receive a perishable wreath, but we an imperishable. [26]Well, I do not run aimlessly, I do not box as one beating the air; [27]but I pommel my body and subdue it, lest after preaching to others I myself should be disqualified.

10 I want you to know, brethren, that our fathers were all under the cloud, and all passed through the sea, [2]and all were baptized into Moses in the cloud and in the sea, [3]and all ate the same supernatural food [4]and all drank the same supernatural drink. For they drank from the supernatural Rock which followed them, and the Rock was Christ. [5]Nevertheless with most of them God was not pleased; for they were overthrown in the wilderness.

6 Now these things are warnings for us, not to desire evil as they did. [7]Do not be idolaters as some of them were; as it is written, "The people sat down to eat and drink and rose up to dance." [8]We must not indulge in immorality as some of them did, and twenty-three thousand fell in a single day. [9]We must not put the Lord to the test, as some of them did and were

destroyed by serpents; [10] nor grumble, as some of them did and were destroyed by the Destroyer. [11]Now these things happened to them as a warning, but they were written down for our instruction, upon whom the end of the ages has come. [12]Therefore let any one who thinks that he stands take heed lest he fall. [13]No temptation has overtaken you that is not common to man. God is faithful, and he will not let you be tempted beyond your strength, but with the temptation will also provide the way of escape, that you may be able to endure it.

14 Therefore, my beloved, shun the worship of idols. [15]I speak as to sensible men; judge for yourselves what I say. [16]The cup of blessing which we bless, is it not a participation in the blood of Christ? The bread which we break, is it not a participation in the body of Christ? [17]Because there is one bread, we who are many are one body, for we all partake of the one bread. [18]Consider the practice of Israel; are not those who eat the sacrifices partners in the altar? [19]What do I imply then? That food offered to idols is anything, or that an idol is anything? [20]No, I imply that what pagans sacrifice they offer to demons and not to God. I do not want you to be partners with demons. [21]You cannot drink the cup of the Lord and the cup of demons. You cannot partake of the table of the Lord and the table of demons. [22]Shall we provoke the Lord to jealousy? Are we stronger than he?

23 "All things are lawful," but not all things are helpful. "All things are lawful," but not all things build up. [24]Let no one seek his own good, but the good of his neighbor. [25]Eat whatever is sold in the meat market without raising any question on the ground of conscience. [26]For "the earth is the Lord's, and everything in it." [27]If one of the unbelievers invites you to dinner and you are disposed to go, eat whatever is set before you without raising any question on the ground of conscience. [28](But if some one says to you, "This has been offered in sacrifice," then out of consideration for the man who informed you, and for conscience' sake—[29]I mean his conscience, not

yours—do not eat it.) For why should my liberty be determined by another man's scruples? [30]If I partake with thankfulness, why am I denounced because of that for which I give thanks?

31 So, whether you eat or drink, or whatever you do, do all to the glory of God. [32]Give no offense to Jews or to Greeks or to the church of God, [33]just as I try to please all men in everything I do, not seeking my own advantage, but that of many, that they may be

11 saved, [1]Be imitators of me, as I am of Christ.

THE AGORA AT CORINTH c. A.D. 50

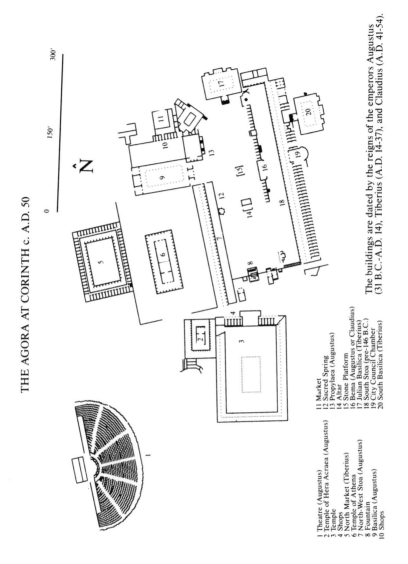

1 Theatre (Augustus)
2 Temple of Hera Acraea (Augustus)
3 Temple
4 Shops
5 North Market (Tiberius)
6 Temple of Athena
7 North-West Stoa (Augustus)
8 Fountain
9 Basilica (Augustus)
10 Shops

11 Market
12 Sacred Spring
13 Propylaea (Augustus)
14 Altar
15 Stone Platform
16 Bema (Augustus or Claudius)
17 Julian Basilica (Tiberius)
18 South Stoa (pre-146 B.C.)
19 City Council Chamber
20 South Basilica (Tiberius)

The buildings are dated by the reigns of the emperors Augustus (31 B.C.–A.D. 14), Tiberius (A.D. 14-37), and Claudius (A.D. 41-54).

fices directed that the donors of the meat share the offering "with the god," as something of a meal together. For all this, there was still an excess of meat remaining from the sacrifices. The solution was to put the meat back into the meat markets to be sold in the next days.

Now if Christian A were invited to Christian B's house for dinner, at which meat is served, Christian A might correctly surmise that this meat had, the day before, been part of a sacrifice to a god, to a false god which challenged the true and only God to whom Christian A had committed himself. If Christian A were of a certain kind of mind, he might well balk at what is put before him, thinking that he would be betraying the true God by partaking of something used in false or idol worship. Christian B, however, obviously thought that the meat was compatible with his belief in the one and true God, for, first of all, the god to whom the meat had been offered was really "no-god," and, second, it had been "secularized" again by its having been put back in the ordinary meat market. In short, Christian A thinks it a sin if he eats the meat; Christian B refuses to think of it that way and insists on serving it in accord with his conviction. Hence a double difficulty is put before Paul: first, is it a sin to eat the meat, and, second, how are these two Christians to get along if one does not accept Paul's decision?

Paul does not waste much time in affirming that the meat can be eaten without sin, for meat cannot be called "sacred" if the gods to whom it is offered do not exist. Paul spends a great deal of time in healing the disunity brought about by the unyielding positions taken by Christians A and B. But before explaining Paul's way of healing this rupture, let us look at the second situation which causes the second part of the main problem, "eating meat which *is being* offered to idols."

Many Christian converts in Corinth maintained friendships with pagans; as is clear from Chapter 7, some marriages were composed of Christian and non-Christian spouses. In the social life which continued after conversion to Christ, there were a number of occasions in which gatherings would include not only normal social events such as a dinner, but also sacrifice to gods, whether those who protect the house or others. On these occasions, which included sacrifice of meat to an idol, the Christian was faced with the problem: May I eat meat, the eating of which indicates that I am sharing in the worship of a god, the worship going on around me at this very table?

So, then, we have two kinds of problems concerning meat offered to idols, and a particularly unpleasant effect resulting from a difference of conscience between Christian A and Christian B about eating meat *previously* offered to idols. I have already indicated Paul's rather uncomplicated resolution of the question: May I eat meat that has earlier been offered to idols? Both Chapter 8, verses 4–6, and Chapter 10, verses 23–30, argue Paul's viewpoint; I plan to refer to the verses of Chapter 10 in more detail and will discuss his advice (found in Chapter 10, verses 1–22) about the second question: May I eat meat that is now being offered to idols? Right now let us look at the way in which Paul tries to bring back into unity Christian A and Christian B.

Resolution of Two Christian Viewpoints

The second half of Chapter 8 (vv 7–13) and all of Chapter 9 are aimed at re-establishing the relationship of charity that should exist between Christian A and Christian B; the amount Paul writes to achieve this aim is witness enough to the worry their disputing has caused him. The essence of Paul's resolution of the dispute rests in the fact that Christian A thinks it sinful if he eats meat earlier offered to idols, whereas Christian B thinks it no sin to eat such meat or not eat it; thus, Christian A is involved in sin, or so he believes. Paul first makes clear (8:4–5,8; 10:25–27) that eating meat already offered to idols is not sinful. But then he asks Christian B, who knows the truth about such eating of meat, to forego the exercise of his conviction so as not to be the cause of Christian A's sinning. Christian A is recognized by Paul as both in error about the eating of the meat and weak; Christian B is admittedly right in his judgment and strong. But since there is sin involved

for Christian A if he eats the meat, Christian B is asked to do all
he can not to be an occasion or cause of sin for Christian A. That
Christian A should be educated to the proper judgment about the
meat is surely the fuller solution to the problem; but in an emer-
gency such as this, and with Paul so distant and the need for immediate remedy so great, Paul's advice seems reasonable. One
should recognize the full circumstances of this problem, for they
all suggest the solution Paul writes to Corinth; if the circumstances
change, one cannot be so certain that what Paul suggests here is
to be applied to the new set of circumstances. Or better, love and
unity should always be goals to achieve in any dispute, but it is
not always clear that the proper means to harmony is the giving
up of the exercise of one's convictions.

   Not to eat the meat is, in this case, the advice of Paul, in order
to avoid pressuring a fellow Christian to sin. Such an advice is bol-
stered, Paul hopes, by first admitting quite honestly the existence of
the rights, of many rights in all kinds of lives, and then by citing his
own example of giving up the exercise of his rights, both in regard
to the Corinthians and in regard to "all men." In this way Paul hopes
to show that he who asks Christian B not to eat the meat is one who
himself has made sacrifices, and great sacrifices at that, for many people and for many years.

Rights and Freedom

   Chapter 9 is filled both with the claims to rights, to what is
one's due, and with the sacrifice of Paul who made himself even a
slave for everyone; in his famous words, he "made himself all
things to all men" to achieve their good (9:22). Chapter 9, verse
5, reveals that others had wives with them in their missionizing
activities; is Paul suggesting here that he did not have a wife,
though he had a right to, as a way of spending all his life solely
for the benefit of his audiences and converts? Paul, in brief, was
willing to give up so much of himself to save others, to sacrifice

his ways of thinking and his habits to become like others, to accept their mind-frame, in order to bring them happiness. It is this which Paul urges upon the "stronger" Christian, a sacrifice for the well-being of his brother. Paul and Christian B are to imitate only one runner in a race, the winner. In this analogy, to lose the race is not to give as much as did the winner; Paul wants his fellow Christians to love fully, totally.

Let us refer to verse 23 of Chapter 10 for a moment. Once again we meet up with the principle, "There are no forbidden things for me," a principle which had appeared earlier in this letter, as the principle by which one tried to argue to the licitness of fornication (6:12). Evidently, there was some strong teaching in Corinth in the direction of complete freedom, so that one felt there was nothing one could not do. Perhaps this was a misunderstanding of the freedom Christians thought they had when they were told they were free from the law (where only certain aspects of the Mosaic law were intended); or perhaps the freedom certain other groups claimed because of their religious or philosophical understandings of man who knows the one truth which will save—perhaps their knowledge of one truth meant that they could do anything in their lives and not worry that they would lose the salvation their "special knowledge" assured. Whatever the source of this undiscriminating freedom, Paul suggests here, as he did in Chapter 6, verse 12, that freedom is limited. In accord with his present argument, he notes that the limitations put on freedom are that good should come out of the exercise of freedom (and here he means good for the neighbor) and that freedom should build or make grow (not destroy or stunt growth). Thus, he can warmly encourage his readers: "Let no one look for his own advantage, but for the advantage of his neighbor" (10:24).

True Knowledge

Paul, then, has offered his advice both as to the legitimacy of eating meat that has earlier been offered to idols and as to the way in which Christian B should heal the ruptured relationship with Christian A. It is in light of his advice to Christian B that I would now like to make reference to the first three verses of Chapter 8. As beginning verses they are puzzling and seem in no way to lead one smoothly into the eventual discussion of Chapters 8 through 10. But Paul already from the start has on his mind what apparently was the attitude of Christian B, which in part accounted for his being at loggerheads with Christian A. Evidently Christian B justified his separation from Christian A on the grounds that "he has knowledge" (8:1), i.e., he knows what is right and has every right to live by it. Paul counters, in the second half of the verse, with the distinction that knowledge (without love) simply puffs up, whereas love actually builds. He is offering here two effects of causes; the first effect is something made big all right, but it is simply big because it is made so by air, like a balloon, whereas the second effect (of love) truly builds something solid, like a building. Paul follows this distinction with a second observation, that one should not be presumed to know as he should, just because he thinks he knows something. Paul is implying here that "knowing as one should know" means "knowledge that helps to love"; until such a knowledge is attained, one cannot really be said to "know" anything. In accord with the first verse, knowledge that does not help one to love does not really build anything. Finally, in thinking of a knowledge that builds, of a knowledge that ends in love, Paul is led to his expression in verse 3. The Old Testament had used a number of terms to indicate God's love for human beings: to turn one's face toward, to look upon, to hear. Another of these terms was "to know," as "God recognizes me, God acknowledges me, God knows me." In this phrasing, God's "knowing me" means that God "loves me." Now, if God loves a person, he gives that person the greatest of his gifts, the ability to love God in return; no one else can make me love God. Thus, if a person loves God, it is due to God's love for him; or, as verse 3 says it, no one loves God without God first "knowing" him. Paul replaces the usual word "loving," however, with the word "knowing," because love is the true flowering or perfection of knowledge; in God's case, his knowing an individual not only created that person (an act of love), but ended in the person's being able to love in return—a truly glorious result of the "knowledge that builds."

Sharing in Idolatry

We have seen how Paul resolves the question of eating meat that has been sacrificed to idols and how he tries to bring disputing Christians to harmony and peace; let us now note how he responds to the problem involved in eating meat as it is being offered to false gods. Verses 1 through 13 are Paul's introduction to his answer; verses 14 through 22 are the answer proper. Let us look first at the latter verses, 14 through 22.

The basic argument of Paul, by which he advises against eating meat which is presently being offered to idols, is that one is sharing in idolatry by sharing this meat. He uses two examples to support his argument. First, the experience of the Corinthian Christians is that their own sharing in the cup and the bread of the community Eucharist is a sharing in the body and blood of Christ; second, the Israelite communion sacrifices—those offered in the temple in Jerusalem to Yahweh, and which the offerers eat as a symbol of feasting with Yahweh who accepts their gifts and "shares" with them—are a sign of union with Yahweh. In both cases, the communion in food is an admission of the Lordship of the ones with whom the believers share their food; the communion is in reality an act of worship. By extension, then, to share in communion with an idol is to admit the lordship of that idol. One may suggest (as does Paul in verse 19) that the idol is not a real being and that the food is therefore not really consecrated; yet, Paul argues that, though the suggestion is valid, one must realize that the false idol is really a front for a true, real demon. It is the demon that has won over the worshiper to worship the demon through the image of the false idol. It is to this reality, the demon, that the Christian must not give gifts; it is with this reality that the Christian must not share food, for the Christian professes union with only one Lord. Thus, sharing in the eating of meat being offered to idols is wrong. There is no provision made for the argument that, though I share in the meal, I do not intend thereby to worship a false god, but only wish to keep friendship with my friend—nor is it clear to me precisely how Paul would handle this argument.

To reach this advice not to eat meat being offered to idols, Paul cites a series of incidents which occurred in the times of ancient Israel and which serve as a warning and a lesson (v 11) so that one be careful not to fall into idol worship. Indeed, these incidents, as narrated in the Old Testament, are stories of an Israel which understood itself to be "chosen," yet suffered extreme penalties for its infidelity and idolatry. The parallel for which Paul is reaching is clear: just as God's love for Israel did not prevent his punishing Israel severely for idolatry, so Christians who participate in services of idol worship cannot count on God's deep love to save them from punishment. (Paul hastens to add, however, that whatever the trial or temptation, whether to idol worship or to even greater dangers, God will not fail to provide a way out of it and strength to put up with it. Paul does not explain how God will involve himself so energetically in the temptations or trials of Christians, but his understanding of who God is gives him absolute confidence in God's interventions.)

More concretely, we can see verses 1 through 4 as the verses which reveal the special love God had for Israel; with verse 5 begins the recital of God's punishments, even to his beloved for sins of desire for forbidden things (v 6), of idolatry (v 7), of sexual immorality (v 8), of testing the Lord (v 9), of complaining against the Lord (v 10). The Christian, who lives at the end of the ages leading up to the

---

TALMUDIC STORY ABOUT THE ROCK
WHICH FOLLOWED THE JEWS
FOR FORTY YEARS IN THE DESERT:

"The rock-spring went up the mountains with the Israelites and descended with them into the valleys; where Israel rested, there did the rock-spring rest . . . "

TSukka 3:11f.

Strack, Herman and Billerbeck, Paul. *Kommentar zum Neuen Testament aus Talmud und Midrasch*, Vol. 3, München, 1954, p. 406.

---

completion of the Old Testament, can learn much from the way God approached sin in the ages past.

The Divine Response to Sins of Ancient Israel

Within Chapter 10, verses 1 through 10, there are three remarks of Paul which deserve a moment's comment. First, Paul's way of speaking about the exodus (vv 1–4b) is couched in terms that remind the reader of his own Christian baptism and Eucharist; the Christian is the one who fulfills the exodus of freedom and the one who is strengthened by the food and drink given by God for strength on the journey to the promised land of God's kingdom. By describing Israel's exodus in this Christian way, Paul emphasizes the chosenness of both Israel and Christianity.

Second, Paul notes that the rock, from which water miraculously flowed for the Israelites (cf Num 20:1–13) at Kadesh, followed the Israelites wherever they went in the desert. What appears to be a bizarre understanding of the Old Testament by rabbis of Paul's time is really meant to underscore the protective love of God for Israel: he would provide water for them always, and he would provide not only food and drink for their bodies, but his word as the food and drink of their souls as well. Now, since everything in the Old Testament is, in principle at least, a sign or teaching about the eventual new age, the lesson of the food and drink miraculously given in the desert must truly concern and foretell the true Food and Drink of God's love, which for the Christian is Christ. Thus, Paul can say that, properly understood, the rock is Christ, the completion of the saving rock of the desert and therefore somehow already contained in it.

Third, verse 7 notes that on one occasion the Israelites sat down to eat and drink and rose up to play; in most modern translations this description of Israel is rightly in italics or quotation marks, for it is taken from the Old Testament (Ex 32:6). One must realize that eating, drinking and playing are, in the exodus story, signs of Israel's having fallen away from Yahweh and now sharing festively in worship of the golden calf. In this context, eating, drinking and playing are condemned.

We have seen all that Paul has to offer on the subject of meat offered to idols and on the subject of sacrifice of the exercise of one's rights for the sake of charity. Paul concludes his remarks by a reminder that whatever one does, even eating and drinking, one does with God's will in mind, i.e., with love toward one's neighbor and in worship of the true God. As he did so extensively in Chapter 9, Paul offers himself as a model for the Corinthians; he does this because he sees himself as modeled on Christ. Ultimately, then, the model is Jesus, even for those who never knew him. It is the function of Paul to mediate Jesus to these new converts; that Paul thinks of himself as the link between Christ and the Corinthian Christians goes far in explaining why Paul entered so thoroughly and energetically into the problems of the Corinthian Christian community.

STUDY QUESTIONS

1. What twofold problem about meat faced Paul in Corinth? Does Paul allow Christians to eat meat offered at an earlier date to pagan idols? On what grounds?

2. Is it right to conclude from Paul's advice to Christian B that one should always give up the exercise of one's rights and convictions? Why is Paul right to ask it here, but might not be right to ask it elsewhere?

3. Paul admits that humans and animals have rights, but how does he argue this? By what critieria has Paul demanded/not demanded that his own rights be respected?

4. By what is freedom limited?

5. Explain how vv. 1–3 of Chapter 8 serve to introduce us to Paul's solution to the problem between Christian A and Christian B.

6 Explain why Paul opposes eating meat as it is being offered to idols.

7 Using Chapter 10, vv. 1–10, explain how St. Paul makes use of the Old Testament.

8. Why does Paul suggest himself as a model for the Corinthians?

Seventh Problem:
Women Not Covering Their
Heads at Worship (11:2–16)

The next question which Paul is asked to address has to do, not with teachings about God or Christ nor with teachings about the moral life, but with custom, specifically the tradition of a woman covering her head when she prays publicly or prophesies. By introducing this problem as one which is concerned with "traditions as I passed them on to you" (11:2), Paul apparently refers to traditions which come from the early or first Christian churches and which have a Palestinian rather than a Greek character. In the tradition of Israel, taken over by the first (Jewish) Christians, there was clear separation of men from women at worship, even as one finds today in Moslem mosques and at prayer at the Western Wall of Jerusalem among Jews. In the first century, women clearly could not approach as close as could men to the holy of holies in the temple of Jerusalem; in synagogues, too, there was clear distinction between men and women. It is this "tradition" which Paul has passed on to Christians in Corinth, some of whom may well have been Jewish converts and thus used to the synagogue manner, but others of whom may well have known no such tradition as pagans and bridled under it—particularly in view of the overall tensions which seem now to plague the Christian community. Paul's long-distance letter tries to solve the problem which lends its own ammunition to the fragmentation of the community; he does this by trying to maintain the tradition of the earlier, semitic churches. Let us see what arguments he suggests to support this tradition of women covering their heads at public prayer and prophecy.

Scripture Text

2 I commend you because you remember me in everything and maintain the traditions even as I have delivered them to you. [3]But I want you to understand that the head of every man is Christ, the head of a woman is her husband, and the head of Christ is God. [4]Any man who prays or prophesies with his head covered dishonors his head, [5]but any woman who prays or prophesies with her head unveiled dishonors her head—it is the same as if her head were shaven. [6]For if a woman will not veil herself, then she should cut off her hair; but if it is disgraceful for a woman to be shorn or shaven, let her wear a veil. [7]For a man ought not to cover his head, since he is the image and glory of God; but woman is the glory of man. [8](For man was not made from woman, but woman from man. [9]Neither was man created for woman, but woman for man.) [10]That is why a woman ought to have a veil on her head, because of the angels. [11](Nevertheless, in the Lord woman is not independent of man nor man of woman; [12]for as woman was made from man, so man is now born of woman. And all things are from God.) [13]Judge for yourselves; is it proper for a woman to pray to God with her head uncovered? [14]Does not nature itself teach you that for a man to wear long hair is degrading to him, [15]but if a woman has long hair, it is her pride? For her hair is given to her for a covering. [16]If any one is disposed to be contentious, we recognize no other practice, nor do the churches of God.

It is not clear whether or not Paul is coming up with arguments which he creates at the moment or are part of the thinking which justified the tradition for a long period of time. Whatever the case, it is clear that Paul's first effort is, as is so customary with him, to search the Old Testament for guidance. There he finds, in the Genesis story of creation, the *distinction* made between man and woman and the implication that man, from whom and for whom came woman, is woman's *head*. He also finds written there that man is the *image* of God *and* God's *glory;* woman is not so fully described. With these three elements in place—distinction, head, and image-glory—Paul concludes, first, that there has to be some way of visibly distinguishing man from woman (at public prayer), second, that this distinction cannot be shown by man covering his head, for to cover the head of the man is to show disrespect for his imaging and reflecting God and his glory, and, third, that, since woman must be distinct from man who cannot cover his head, it is only logical that the woman cover her head at prayer. Another way of saying this is that because man is obliged to pray with his head uncovered, woman, to show her distinction from man and her origin from him, must cover her head.

But the argument drawn from man's "headship" at creation can be concluded in a slightly different way: if a woman will not cover her head, she should have her hair cut off. Paul does not intend this literally, but he means to emphasize by it that the woman who shames her head (he means principally "her husband," but includes with the word her own "physical head") might as well shame her "physical head," too; if she shames her head by leaving it uncovered, why should she then protect the honor of her head by leaving it covered? And to deny man as the source and reason for her being is implied in her not covering her head at public prayer.

Disrespect for one's lord or head in public functions must imply disorder, and to allow disorder into the public prayer meetings of the Christian community is to offend the angels who were the protectors of proper order in the worship of Yahweh. No doubt this appeal to the presence of those who traditionally in Old Testament times were models for and guardians of proper worship of Yahweh is an appeal to another of the traditions coming from the earliest (Jewish) Christians.

A final argument in favor of women covering their heads when praying and prophesying publicly is that argument drawn from "nature." By "nature" Paul does not mean the metaphysical entity of an Aristotle or an Aquinas, nor does he mean simply custom, i.e., the current fashion of wearing hair. He rather means that woman traditionally has hair longer than man, no matter what she (or he) might do with it in a particular culture. His argument is not to establish this meaning of nature, however; he takes it for granted and argues from it in a rather clever way. He concludes that woman is really meant to cover her head, because that is the import of having such long hair to begin with. One might argue that if she has hair of such abundance as to cover her head, then why must she cover it again with a veil? But that is to misunderstand the sign nature gives: by giving her such hair, nature is saying that she should by all means have her head covered and that the hair covering is not enough; a veil is in order.

Such are the arguments which Paul has given on behalf of women covering their heads in public prayer and prophecy. It is quite clear that Paul's opinion has been, if not the deciding factor, then at least the one written support of a tradition which has been the norm in many scripture-based churches for many hundreds of years. Yet, it is equally clear that for most all of these churches the tradition has been abandoned; is this a direct challenge to the advice and reasoning of Paul in this letter?

Paul Doubts His Own Arguments?

I would suggest that Paul himself is unsure as to whether or not his arguments would be convincing, as to whether or not one culture's traditions would really work in another culture. Moreover, if anyone was sensitive to and favorable toward the adaptation of worship of the true God through Christ, it was Paul. The reason I think Paul is unsure about the attractiveness of his arguments lies in the consideration of a few of his verses and in the overall nature of the letter.

Verses which seem out of place in the Pauline argument are verse 11 and verse 12a. I say they are out of place because they dilute the force of Paul's argument that man is the head of woman. Perhaps all they do is avoid a misunderstanding of what man's headship is: he is head only in the sense that woman originated from man and was made as companion of man. But companion does not automatically imply subordination or inequality, and origin is not a very good kind of argument, for, as verses 11 and 12a admit, after Adam and Eve, every man is born from woman. Thus, the Genesis story, though it certainly witnesses to the distinction of woman and man, does little to argue against the age-long reality of man's dependence upon woman as his source of life. Why does Paul bring up this statement of man's dependence upon woman? I think the answer lies in Paul's own honesty with himself, that while he tries to bring peace and unity to the community of Corinthian Christians through a choice in favor of the tradition, he honestly concedes a certain limitedness or imperfection to his argument.

Added to this hesitancy of Paul at verses 11 and 12a is Paul's rather unusual closing appeal to "custom, among us and among the other churches of God" (v 16). This last statement, as I read it, is practically an admission that the arguments of the first fifteen verses will be unconvincing. I am not sure they are convincing to Paul, but it is certain to me that Paul knew they were unconvincing to those raised in non-Jewish traditions. It is this knowledge which leads Paul to close his discussion of this matter by an appeal to "custom" after a long appeal to reason.

The real question becomes, then: Why did Paul choose to uphold a tradition which he realized made little sense to a person outside the Old Testament tradition? For all Paul's argument, I think he recognizes this problem as of minor importance and certainly not the equal of the problems, such as incest and fornication, we have seen treated earlier. Given the relative insignificance of the problem, Paul does recognize it as a factor contributing to the overall destruction of the Christian community, and so he is eager and anxious to resolve it; in other words, it is in one sense a small thing Paul is asking of those who want to pray or prophesy with heads uncovered, and yet it is made big enough to demand conformity to tradition because of its contribution to the radical community division occurring because of at least nine other points of tension. To put it another way, I am not so sure just what Paul's ultimate recommendation would have been about this disagreement at Corinth, if it were the only problem there.

But Paul did come down on the side of tradition. This may not, however, have been out of blind preference for tradition, but it may have been a choice which he thought most likely to make peace at Corinth. Freedom where freedom was legitimate was a hope Paul always encouraged, but his support of a way of acting so out of line with the rest of the churches was less prudent than encouragement to "custom."

In short, then, there are enough indications (the tense situation in the Corinthian church, Paul's longing for peace and unity, the relatively small sacrifices asked of some, the hesitancies in Paul's own text about his solution) to explain why Paul chose to advise obedience to custom and why the advice was not so firmly given that it could not be changed. It was after all a matter, not of doctrine or morals, but of "custom."

STUDY QUESTIONS

1. Why are some Christians accustomed to having women pray publicly or prophesy with their heads covered?
2. How does Paul argue from the Old Testament that a woman must pray publicly and prophesy with her head covered?

3. That a woman prays publicly with head uncovered shames her husband and disturbs angels. Why?

4. In what sense is man not "head" of woman, but dependent upon her?

5. Why does Paul ultimately appeal to custom as his final statement?

10

Eighth Problem:
A Lack of Appreciation of
the Holy Eucharist (11:17–34)

Paul has spoken of one problem occurring at meetings of public prayer; now he directs his attention to another problem (or, better, two problems) plaguing the worship of Christians. It seems that, while attending the gathering of Christians to perform the Eucharist, such a degree of feasting is enjoyed by some that, first, they lose awareness of the significance of the Eucharist which they eat and drink, and, second, they separate themselves from those poorer Christians who do not have much food or drink to enjoy. But to understand these abuses, one must be alerted to the circumstances in which the early Christians celebrated their Eucharist.

There were no churches in early Christianity, but people met in the house of a Christian who generously offered to sponsor a Eucharist. But to hold a eucharistic celebration in those days was to hold, in fact, two meals: the spiritual, eucharistic meal and a regular meal of food and drink. This regular or normal type of meal actually was held as an introduction to or preparation for the spiritual meal of the Eucharist. Judging it all from the best of intentions, one could say that the initial gathering for a meal was a meal of friendship shared by those committed to Christ, that this expression of charity shared was a good way of entering into the significance of the eucharistic meal to follow immediately.

One circumstance which archeology has pointed up is the layout

17 But in the following instructions I do not commend you, because when you come together it is not for the better but for the worse. [18]For, in the first place, when you assemble as a church, I hear that there are divisions among you; and I partly believe it, [19]for there must be factions among you in order that those who are genuine among you may be recognized. [20]When you meet together, it is not the Lord's supper that you eat. [21]For in eating, each one goes ahead with his own meal, and one is hungry and another is drunk. [22]What! Do you not have houses to eat and drink in? Or do you despise the church of God and humiliate those who have nothing? What shall I say to you? Shall I commend you in this? No, I will not.

23 For I received from the Lord what I also delivered to you, that the Lord Jesus on the night when he was betrayed took bread, [24]and when he had given thanks, he broke it, and said, "This is my body which is for you. Do this in remembrance of me." [25]In the same way also the cup, after supper, saying, "This cup is the new covenant in my blood. Do this, as often as you drink it, in remembrance of me." [26]For as often as you eat this bread and drink the cup, you proclaim the Lord's death until he comes.

27 Whoever, therefore, eats the bread or drinks the cup of the Lord in an unworthy manner will be guilty of profaning the body and blood of the Lord. [28]Let a man examine himself, and so eat of the bread and drink of the cup. [29]For any one who eats and drinks without discerning the body eats and drinks judgment upon himself. [30]That is why many of you are weak and ill, and some have died. [31]But if we judged ourselves truly, we should not be judged. [32]But when we are judged by

the Lord, we are chastened so that we may not be condemned along with the world.

33 So then, my brethren, when you come together to eat, wait for one another—[34]if any one is hungry, let him eat at home—lest you come together to be condemned. About the other things I will give directions when I come.

of what we might call a "normal-sized" house in Corinth. That is, a Corinthian house of this period would not normally have a room large enough to hold more than fifteen people; if the Christian community were larger than that, it would have spilled over into an adjacent room or courtyard (and if the community were still larger, it would have had to divide itself, with a part remaining in the original house and another part going to a second house). I give this description to suggest why even the physical arrangements of the place of celebration might lead to making distinctions between those who got a place in the main room of the house and those who got a place in the adjacent room or courtyard.

Another circumstance to be considered is this, that the one who offered his or her house for this twofold meal was not thereby expected to provide the food and drink of the first or regular-type, festive meal. Rather, each Christian would provide his own food and drink. This practice accounts for the fact that some Christians have much more to eat and to drink than do others.

Given these circumstances, certain abuses have arisen at these meals in Corinth. First, those who have more than others do not have the sensitivity to realize that the so-called meal of charity is no longer such, for the poor among them are finished long before the wealthier Christians, and an embarrassment is created which hardly encourages charity and unity. Second, plenty of drink to some meant to drink excessively, to the point, Paul is told, that they do not realize the meaning of the eucharistic meal immediately following upon their festive drinking. It is to these two abuses that Paul must address himself now.

Gather Only for the Eucharist

Paul's solution to the problem arising from the disparity of food among the Christians is radical and quite possibly standard-setting. It is radical in that he asks the Christians to eat the ordinary, festive meal at their own home and no longer in the home where the Eucharist will be held. It is quite possibly standard-setting because, though for lack of full documentation we cannot be certain, we never

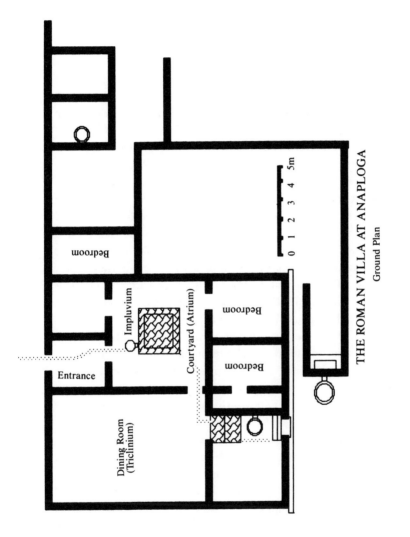

THE ROMAN VILLA AT ANAPLOGA
Ground Plan

Entrance

Dining Room
(Triclinium)

Impluvium

Courtyard (Atrium)

Bedroom

Bedroom

Bedroom

0 1 2 3 4 5m

hear again in Christianity of the practice of having the Eucharist pre-
ceded by a regular-type meal. Such seems to be the effect of Paul's
directive in this letter.

Paul, indeed, was concerned for the unity and charity of the
Christian community, and was not willing to have the misuse of
wealth be a cause for the embarrassment which divides the poor from
the rich. He also, however, turned his attention to the indignity of
receiving the Eucharist in an unworthy, drunken manner. Certainly,
Paul's corrective is right and thoroughly expected. What is of particular value is the series of statements by which Paul discusses the
eucharistic celebration.

First, we have the very significant clause we have seen used once
before (at 7:10, regarding divorce): "what I received from the Lord"
(11:23). Thus, we are given here something which was not created
by the earliest Christians, but something traceable back to Christ
himself; as a comparison of the words of consecration, as they appear
in Matthew, Mark, Luke and Paul, will show, we are not certain as
to the exact wording Jesus used, but the essential elements of the
formulas are what should be ascribed to him.

Second, Paul's use of the pair of words, "received—handed on,"
is a formal indication for those who recognize it of his being simply
a conduit through which tradition passes; rabbis would use these
words when emphasizing that what they were teaching was not
theirs, but that they were merely acting as intermediaries for the true
source of the teaching and changed it in no way.

Third, Paul notes elements of the Last Supper which will be part
of the Gospels to be written from ten to thirty years after this First
Letter to the Corinthians: "on the same night on which he was betrayed," "took some bread, gave thanks to God, broke it and said,"
"in the same way after supper." Thus, what the Gospels report to
third-generation Christians is clearly visible as the tradition given to
second-generation Christians, a tradition handed down from a still
earlier Christian worshiping community.

The Significance of the Eucharist Made Clear

As far as significance goes, Paul recognizes the bread as the "body which is for you," clearly an understanding of the crucifixion as something done for these Corinthian Christians. The wine is the "blood of the new covenant," which recalls the agreement by which the Israelites in the desert were formally made God's people and he their God through a sprinkling of blood on the seat of mercy (which represents God) and on the people. This agreement or covenant (made through Moses at Mount Sinai) is the basis for calling to mind a new covenant, a new agreement whereby God has taken for himself a new people and this new people has accepted God as theirs, all through the sprinkling of a new blood, the blood of Jesus. This covenant or agreement is made with the Corinthians.

Since both the bread become body and the wine become blood are remembered in their sacrificial character, it is logical for Paul to think of the reception of these elements as a witness or proclamation of death, Jesus' death, the death "for others." And there is little doubt, in view of Paul's way of speaking, that he considers the bread and wine as Christ's body and blood.

Finally, Paul reverts to a way of thinking which was typical of the Old Testament. That is to say, often when one event follows upon another, there is seen by those who believe in God's active role in events which succeed each other a causal connection; in Paul's discussion here, he sees a causal link between the dishonor done to the body and blood of Christ and sickness, even death, in the community. It is not always easy to agree with the Old Testament and Paul in assigning causes to certain events, but there is in support of their claim the argument of "fittingness," that the event is fittingly described as the effect of an earlier event or cause. Thus, in this case it is "fitting" to think of sickness and death as just and fair punishment for dishonoring the body and blood of Jesus.

It is also noteworthy that throughout this discussion Paul has consistently avoided the word "Christ" and pervasively used the word "Lord." In doing this he gives witness to the title by which Jesus was addressed and spoken of particularly at the liturgies of the Christians.

Paul, then, has given his advice about the abuses which upset the community worship, abuses which abet the factions he notes in verse 18, factions which may be formed along the lines of those discussed in his first four chapters. It becomes increasingly clear as this letter progresses how divided the community must have been and often over matters which we would not consider trivial; one can, in realizing this, understand better the anxiety and worry which account for the way in which Paul addresses problems and those who cause them.

STUDY QUESTIONS

1. What is the background to the problems developing at Eucharistic celebrations?

2. How does Paul limit the harmful effects of wealth as they might affect the poor attending the Eucharistic worship?

3. What are important aspects of Paul's reference to the traditions about the Eucharist?

4. Explain the "body which is for you," "the blood of the new covenant."

5. Is sickness and death reasonably attributable to misuse of Christ's body and blood?

11

Ninth Problem:
Gifts of the Holy Spirit (12:1–14:40)

One of the great blessings bestowed on this early Christian community in Corinth was the blessing of spiritual gifts, gifts given by the Holy Spirit. Some of these gifts are: preaching with wisdom, teaching, special faith, healing, miracle-working, prophecy, discernment of spirits, speaking in tongues, interpreting the speaking in tongues. If these gifts are from the Holy Spirit, they clearly are meant for good; yet, it is clear that something is amiss in Corinth regarding them, and Paul must provide cures for the abuses and misconceptions about these gifts (particularly that of the gift of speaking in tongues) lest the misuse of them further destroy the unity of the Christian community.

Chapters 12, 13 and 14 are dedicated to resolving the problems connected with the gifts from the Spirit. The basic line of logic Paul follows is, first, to emphasize the tendency of these gifts to unity, then to relate these gifts to charity or love of God and neighbor, and, finally, to provide specific ideas and recommendations regarding the use of the gift of speaking in tongues when Christians are gathered in prayer together. It is this threefold scheme—unity, charity, order at prayer meetings—which I will follow here.

Unity Through the Holy Spirit

In 12:4–11 Paul's main goal is to point up the unity inherent in the multiplicity and diversity of these spiritual gifts. He does this in two ways. First, he links the multiplicity and diversity of the gifts

12 Now concerning spiritual gifts, brethren, I do not want you to be uninformed. ²You know that when you were heathen, you were led astray to dumb idols, however you may have been moved. ³Therefore I want you to understand that no one speaking by the Spirit of God ever says "Jesus be cursed!" and no one can say "Jesus is Lord" except by the Holy Spirit.

4 Now there are varieties of gifts, but the same Spirit; ⁵and there are varieties of service, but the same Lord; ⁶and there are varieties of working, but it is the same God who inspires them all in every one. ⁷To each is given the manifestation of the Spirit for the common good. ⁸To one is given through the Spirit the utterance of wisdom, and to another the utterance of knowledge according to the same Spirit, ⁹to another faith by the same Spirit, to another gifts of healing by the one Spirit, ¹⁰to another the working of miracles, to another prophecy, to another the ability to distinguish between spirits, to another various kinds of tongues, to another the interpretation of tongues. ¹¹All these are inspired by one and the same Spirit, who apportions to each one individually as he wills.

12 For just as the body is one and has many members, and all the members of the body, though many, are one body, so it is with Christ. ¹³For by one Spirit we were all baptized into one body—Jews or Greeks, slaves or free—and all were made to drink of one Spirit.

14 For the body does not consist of one member but of many. ¹⁵If the foot should say, "Because I am not a hand, I do not belong to the body," that would not make it any less a part of the body. ¹⁶And if the ear should say, "Because I am not an eye, I do not belong to the body," that would not make it any less a part of the body. ¹⁷If the whole body were an eye, where

would be the hearing? If the whole body were an ear, where would be the sense of smell? [18]But as it is, God arranged the organs in the body, each one of them, as he chose. [19]If all were a single organ, where would the body be? [20]As it is, there are many parts, yet one body. [21]The eye cannot say to the hand, "I have no need of you," nor again the head to the feet, "I have no need of you." [22]On the contrary, the parts of the body which seem to be weaker are indispensable, [23]and those parts of the body which we think less honorable we invest with the greater honor, and our unpresentable parts are treated with greater modesty, [24]which our more presentable parts do not require. But God has so adjusted the body, giving the greater honor to the inferior part, [25]that there may be no discord in the body, but that the members may have the same care for one another. [26]If one member suffers, all suffer together; if one member is honored, all rejoice together.

27 Now you are the body of Christ and individually members of it. [28]And God has appointed in the church first apostles, second prophets, third teachers, then workers of miracles, then healers, helpers, administrators, speakers in various kinds of tongues. [29]Are all apostles? Are all prophets? Are all teachers? Do all work miracles? [30]Do all possess gifts of healing? Do all speak with tongues? Do all interpret? [31]But earnestly desire the higher gifts.

And I will show you a still more excellent way.

13 If I speak in the tongues of men and of angels, but have not love, I am a noisy gong or a clanging cymbal. [2]And if I have prophetic powers, and understand all mysteries and all knowledge, and if I have all faith, so as to remove mountains, but have not love, I am nothing. [3]If I give away all I have, and if I deliver my body to be burned, but have not love, I gain nothing.

4 Love is patient and kind; love is not jealous or boastful; [5]it is not arrogant or rude. Love does not insist on its own way;

it is not irritable or resentful; [6]it does not rejoice at wrong, but rejoices in the right. [7]Love bears all things, believes all things, hopes all things, endures all things.

8 Love never ends; as for prophecies, they will pass away; as for tongues, they will cease; as for knowledge, it will pass away. [9]For our knowledge is imperfect and our prophecy is imperfect; [10]but when the perfect comes, the imperfect will pass away. [11]When I was a child, I spoke like a child, I thought like a child, I reasoned like a child; when I became a man, I gave up childish ways. [12]For now we see in a mirror dimly, but then face to face. Now I know in part; then I shall understand fully, even as I have been fully understood. [13]So faith, hope, love abide, these three; but the greatest of these is love.

14 Make love your aim, and earnestly desire the spiritual gifts, especially that you may prophesy. [2]For one who speaks in a tongue speaks not to men but to God; for no one understands him, but he utters mysteries in the Spirit. [3]On the other hand, he who prophesies speaks to men for their upbuilding and encouragement and consolation. [4]He who speaks in a tongue edifies himself, but he who prophesies edifies the church. [5]Now I want you all to speak in tongues, but even more to prophesy. He who prophesies is greater than he who speaks in tongues, unless some one interprets, so that the church may be edified.

6 Now, brethren, if I come to you speaking in tongues, how shall I benefit you unless I bring you some revelation or knowledge or prophecy or teaching? [7]If even lifeless instruments, such as the flute or the harp, do not give distinct notes, how will any one know what is played? [8]And if the bugle gives an indistinct sound, who will get ready for battle? [9]So with yourselves; if you in a tongue utter speech that is not intelligible, how will any one know what is said? For you will be speaking into the air. [10]There are doubtless many different lan-

guages in the world, and none is without meaning; ¹¹but if I
do not know the meaning of the language, I shall be a foreigner
to the speaker and the speaker a foreigner to me. ¹²So with
yourselves; since you are eager for manifestations of the Spirit,
strive to excel in building up the church.

13 Therefore, he who speaks in a tongue should pray for
the power to interpret. ¹⁴For if I pray in a tongue, my spirit
prays but my mind is unfruitful. ¹⁵What am I to do? I will pray
with the spirit and I will pray with the mind also; I will sing
with the spirit and I will sing with the mind also. ¹⁶Otherwise,
if you bless with the spirit, how can any one in the position of
an outsider say the "Amen" to your thanksgiving when he does
not know what you are saying. ¹⁷For you may give thanks well
enough, but the other man is not edified. ¹⁸I thank God that
I speak in tongues more than you all; ¹⁹nevertheless, in church
I would rather speak five words with my mind, in order to instruct others, than ten thousand words in a tongue.

20 Brethren, do not be children in your thinking; be
babes in evil, but in thinking be mature. ²¹In the law it is written, "By men of strange tongues and by the lips of foreigners
will I speak to this people, and even then they will not listen
to me, says the Lord." ²²Thus, tongues are a sign not for believers but for unbelievers, while prophecy is not for unbelievers but for believers. ²³If, therefore, the whole church assembles
and all speak in tongues, and outsiders or unbelievers enter,
will they not say that you are mad? ²⁴But if all prophesy, and
an unbeliever or outsider enters, he is convicted by all, he is
called to account by all, ²⁵the secrets of his heart are disclosed;
and so, falling on his face, he will worship God and declare that
God is really among you.

26 What then, brethren? When you come together, each
one has a hymn, a lesson, a revelation, a tongue, or an interpretation. Let all things be done for edification. ²⁷If any speak
in a tongue, let there be only two or at most three, and each in

turn; and let one interpret. [2]But if there is no one to interpret, let each of them keep silence in church and speak to himself and to God. [29]Let two or three prophets speak, and let the others weigh what is said. [30]If a revelation is made to another sitting by, let the first be silent. [31]For you can all prophesy one by one, so that all may learn and all be encouraged; [32]and the spirits of prophets are subject to prophets. [33]For God is not a God of confusion but of peace.

As in all the churches of the saints, [34]the women should keep silence in the churches. For they are not permitted to speak, but should be subordinate, as even the law says. [35]If there is anything they desire to know, let them ask their husbands at home. For it is shameful for a woman to speak in church. [36]What! Did the word of God originate with you, or are you the only ones it has reached?

37 If any one thinks that he is a prophet, or spiritual, he should acknowledge that what I am writing to you is a command of the Lord. [38]If any one does not recognize this, he is not recognized. [39]So, my brethren, earnestly desire to prophesy, and do not forbid speaking in tongues; [40]but all things should be done decently and in order.

with one Spirit, so that the one through whom the gifts are given is always the same Person. Similarly, he links the variety of services done by these gifts to one Person, Jesus Christ; all gifts ultimately serve the same Lord. Likewise, the ultimate source, who gives the many gifts through the one Spirit, is one and only one, that is, it is God the Father. Thus, in three different ways the gifts witness to oneness, to unity: to one source (God the Father), to one mediator (Holy Spirit), to one Lord who is served by them (Jesus Christ). One must also add Paul's notion that God is working through these gifts in people; thus, one can see not only oneness of source for these many gifts, and oneness of mediator and of Lord served, but one realizes that the exercise of the varied gifts is really the work of the one, living God. But there is still more to consider. First, every gift is ordained to a good purpose; thus, no matter the variety of gifts, the goal is always ultimately the same, the good of others. Second, as the gifts point to one God, one Spirit, one Lord, so they imply a oneness of plan among God, the Spirit and the Lord; even in this way the multiplicity of gifts suggests oneness.

With verses 12 through 30 Paul introduces a reality which should further help the Corinthians grasp the unity which the gifts of the Spirit foster. It is the reality of the body of Christ, a reality already used in connection with Paul's earlier discussion about fornication/ prostitution (Chapter 6, verse 15). But whereas in that discussion the body of Christ was used to show the significance of being a member of it, in what Paul now writes the body of Christ is used to make understandable the ways in which members of the body serve one another while all are rooted in Christ as his members and create the body as members do. Indeed, it is the exercise of these gifts for the good of one another which preserves a body that moves and lives by Christ's Spirit.

The emphasis in these verses, as in the earlier verses 4 through 11, is argument in the direction of showing unity in the midst of very evident diversity; thus, Paul is not justifying variety, but arguing always to the unity underlying and guiding diversity. The analogy Paul uses concerning the good various limbs do for the entire body and the sensitivity and empathy necessarily found in the limbs of one and the same body—this analogy and its characteristics are clear and should help the Corinthians realize how interdependent they are and how the exercise of their gifts must be understood as gifts for others. Given Paul's approach, a gifted Christian has no grounds to be pompous because he has a gift and another does not, because the gift he has is greater than that of another Christian; the gifts are for the good of others, of the entire community and not for one's ego. It is a grave mistake to think that the Spirit has bestowed this kind of spiritual gift for one's own self; the Christian can only be proud that he is serving others with his gift.

But the analogy of the physical body is replaced by clear reference to the body of Christ. The Christian is not living simply as a member of a group or club or association. The gifts indicate the kind of community that is being fostered by their exercise; apostleship, prophecy, teaching, leadership, healing, miracle-working—all these show that the group is peculiarly developed as the body of Christ. Paul does not here explain just how Christians are the body of Christ, nor how an individual becomes a member of the body. His concern here is to help the Corinthians draw a conclusion about the meaning and purpose of the gifts from the fact that they are indeed the body of Christ, a body which thrives on the use of its members and the members of which draw benefit from the contributions of one another. The fact that one member does not have all the gifts is sign enough of his dependence on the others, all to the health of a vigorous body of Christ.

Paul has taken the reality of the gifts of the Spirit and shows a multiplicity of reasons why they should always be considered and known as unifying. In appearance, they may seem diverse and bewilderingly varied, but the reality is that, as their source is one, so their goal is one: to serve the one Lord, to build up his body, to provide only a good to Christians who otherwise would not be able to rejoice in that good; how dependent Christians are on one another! Such is the will of God by which people are healed through love.

Consideration of Chapter 12, Verses 1–3

Having explained, then, the unity that underlies the gifts and is their fruition, Paul is about to move into the explanation of charity vis-à-vis these spiritual gifts. But before looking at Chapter 13 which deals with charity, it is best to give some explanation of the first three verses of Chapter 12, which in some way are meant to introduce the subject of the gifts. We shall have to look at verses 1, 2 and 3 in some detail in order to understand them well.

The three verses hang together in a visible way through the repeated use of the idea "to know." In verse 1, Paul wants his fellow believers to "know about the gifts." In verse 2 Paul appeals to the personal experience of the Corinthians, "You know that when you were pagans. . . ." In verse 3, Paul draws a conclusion, "And so I want to make you know that. . . ." Verse 1 sets the goal of Chapter 12, which is to give knowledge about the gifts; verse 2 recalls an experience of pagan times, so that in verse 3 new knowledge or understanding may result. Most all of Chapter 12 is instruction about the gifts, but what do verses 2 and 3 have to yield in terms of understanding the gifts?

The experience of the Corinthians before they were Christians is of a compulsion: they "were driven" to idols. Paul means to recall the witness of those who "felt drawn" to idols, in order to show how response to idols is the result of a "kind of possession," the effect of a "kind of being drawn or driven." If the Christians remember this claim, then they should be able to understand a similar claim, namely, that what draws one to Jesus is a movement instilled from the outside, so that one can say he "is driven, drawn" to Jesus. Thus, if Christians profess Jesus as Lord, this profession is due to their being moved or drawn or driven by an external force to profess this. Conversely, no one can, under the influence of a power friendly to Jesus, be moved to curse Jesus. Thus, one kind of experience (in a time of paganism) should help clarify another kind of experience (in a time of Christian belief): if one's worship of idols was owed to a movement felt from outside, so it should be assumed that worship of Jesus is owed to a movement from the outside, specifically, from the Holy Spirit.

Such is the meaning of the first verses, but why is Paul concerned to make this point? I believe Paul begins his discussion about gifts, which undeniably are not given to every Christian, in order to establish the pre-eminent value of every Christian's profession that "Jesus is Lord." Thus, the gifts, which are undoubtedly striking and most useful, are building upon an already existing movement found in each Christian, a proceeding from the Holy Spirit. Thus, every Christian is "driven" to profess Jesus as Lord, even though some Christians are moved also to certain specific good deeds such as healing, speaking in tongues, prophesying. In beginning his discussion of the spiritual gifts this way, Paul is putting them in a proper perspective; no one, in other words, is "better" or "more excellent" because he is moved by the Spirit to this or that action, when all are moved to the essential profession which saves. That Christians should be divided because some are given a particular movement of the Spirit is a false step; all "are driven by the Spirit."

No doubt what is behind the attention given to the wondrous gifts (e.g., speaking in tongues) is the pagan background of the Christians. In those pagan years it was not uncommon to know or participate in religious worship which involved frenzy, whether in speech or in action; a sure sign of "union" with the god was possession by that god, expressed in strange speech and unnatural activity. Perhaps it is to be expected that recent converts would be unduly struck by the forcefulness of Christians speaking in tongues or healing or prophesying and credit those Christians or themselves with a fuller union with God. Paul does not deny the value of the gifts, but he gives them second place to the faith of all Christians in Jesus as Lord. He also, in Chapter 13, shows them a way of life which is better than any of the gifts of the Spirit; to Chapter 13, then, we now turn our attention.

Charity through the Holy Spirit

The love or charity which Paul recommended to the Corinthians in an almost poetical way is not called a gift; it is a way, a way of life. It is not restricted to this or that Christian as is a gift, but it is offered to every Christian. Needless to say, Paul is fervent and enthusiastic about this "way," for it is only in embracing it that the Corinthians will find the unity that is the essence of Christianity and the solution to almost all the problems which are so poignantly reflected in this Pauline letter. Paul, then, is not giving a simple theoretical exposition about the relationship between the Spirit's gifts and charity; he is fighting for the very life of Christianity, a life whose source and goal is love.

In treating of charity or love of God and neighbor, Paul is concerned to make one point, to justify his initial statement that this "way" is superior to all else. He makes his point in three ways: first, a contrast between virtue which is even heroic and charity (vv 1–3); second, a description of the characteristics of charity (vv 4–7); third, a measurement of charity by the criterion or standard of "unendingness," a criterion which says that that is more important and more valuable which lasts longer.

There is little one can say to "clarify" or make "more intelligible" the praise of charity as Paul narrates it; one who practices charity and one who has been the object of true charity have the best understanding of what Paul intends here in these verses. One can only draw attention to the particular concern of Paul to encourage the Corinthian Christians to live this "way," to esteem it as better than all other blessings of God, to let charity have the ultimate influence in all their decisions about God and neighbor. Not only are great virtues meaningless without love; the great gifts and virtues, such as prophecy and knowledge of mysteries, even faith and hope, all will end and the only power which will continue forever is love. Of what value are gifts of the Spirit and faith and hope at a time when only love matters, when it is only love which should continue? If one does not have love then, and if all else has disappeared, what does he have who boasted without love of his "superior" gifts? He has given up what is truly superior for passing things.

The Role of Speaking in Tongues at Prayer Meetings

As Paul moves from his energetic encouragement to love to his advice about the manner in which the particular gift of speaking in tongues should be exercised, he urges the Corinthian Christians once more to want love above all else, but also to hope for the Spirit's gifts (at 12:31 he urged them to aspire to the gifts, even to the highest of them) and especially that of prophecy. Why this sudden selection and attention to prophecy?

Paul is not speaking in purely theoretical or abstract terms, but constantly has his eye on the divisive troubles of the community. In these days, those gifted with the charism of speaking in tongues have so exercised their gift at public prayer meetings that both charity and the order which should flow from it are notably lacking. Paul's ultimate answer to this disorder is a call for order in the exercise of the gifts, an order which is determined by what is best for the preservation and growth of the community in these meetings. But while on the way to ultimately recommending order, Paul shows the relative value of the gift of tongues, especially when compared with a gift such as prophecy. In preparation for this contrast between tongues and prophecy, then, Paul begins his consideration with advice which pointedly singles out prophecy as the preferred gift. Thus, prophecy may not be the greatest gift, but it shows best the lesser value of the gift of tongues.

The benefit of prophecy is put in various ways by Paul; in one statement he says that prophecy "speaks to others, for their betterment, their encouragement, their consolation" (14:3). The gift of tongues, on the other hand, speaks only to God really, for no one else understands what is said; it speaks only about mysterious things which, if there be no one present with the gift of interpretation of tongues, remain completely unintelligible. When one evaluates the benefit the community derives from the gift of tongues, then one can see why Paul emphasizes the relative good it produces; this is the criterion Paul uses to curb the divisive enthusiasm of those with the gift of speaking in tongues.

Value of the Gift of Tongues

But what is the value, even relative, of the gift of tongues? Though it is not Paul's intention to praise this gift very highly, given the circumstances plaguing the Corinthian community at this moment, Paul does give hints about the worth of this gift. First, the gift is a striking witness to the presence of God's Spirit in the gifted one; this in itself is significant and worthwhile, as is any impressive sign of God's presence. And the gift of tongues does impress and astound those who hear the exercise of it. Second, the person so gifted as to speak in tongues is speaking to God and his spirit is praying; this absorption of the person in God is obviously a good, even though in the psychology/anthropology of that time one can say that the mind is "empty" (14:14). Finally, if there is someone with the gift of interpretation of tongues, there can be something intelligible for the rest of the community to share in, and this should be a benefit for the entire assembly. Indeed, Paul admits his esteem for the gift of tongues, for he himself, as gifted with it, has enjoyed it in a more intense form than anyone in Corinth (14:18). There is much good, then, admittedly in this gift of speaking in tongues, but it, like so many other things, must be regulated by the way of love wherein one asks what is for the good of one's neighbor.

Prophecy and Speaking in Tongues

Paul offers two final thoughts (vv 20–25) by which he hopes to encourage a true assessment of the gifts of speaking in tongues and prophecy. His first idea is a reflection on scripture, a process Paul habitually engages in. He sees in a text of Isaiah 28:11–12 (compare, too, Deuteronomy 28:49) the joining of three terms: speaking in foreign languages, the people or nation (= Israel) and "not listening." These three terms are meant by Isaiah to convey the idea that Israel, because she is unfaithful to God and disbelieving, will be spoken to in languages she will not understand. Now Paul, reflecting on Isaiah's message, concludes that "speaking in languages that cannot be understood" belongs to the "unbelieving"; it is something that scripture indicates befits the unbeliever as a sign of his unbelief. But, he implies (though does not write), the Christian community of Corinth is not an unbelieving community, but rather a community of believers; thus "unintelligible tongues" is not for them, but rather the gift of prophecy, the speaking of something intelligible, is befitting them. Thus, scripture is shown to support Paul's preference for prophecy over tongues, for it is the former which will most profit believers.

In this first of his final two arguments, Paul has shown that "speaking in languages foreign to a people" is unbefitting a people which believes; scripture, in fact, had indicated that such unintelligible speech had been God's way of warning or punishing an unfaithful Israel. Now Paul, though using the term "unbeliever" again, strikes up his second argument. Instead of noting the way God has dealt with the unbeliever, he suggests a scene in which an unbeliever or a simple person enters a Christian prayer meeting dominated by the speaking in tongues; what will such a person, who does not know the Spirit who prompts these gifts, think of all this? Paul thinks that such a person will call everyone possessed or frenzied, most of all because he does not understand a word of the "speech" he hears. On the other hand, if an unbeliever enters a prayer meeting in which prophecy dominates, he may be so taken by what he hears *and understands* that he repents and converts to the Lord Jesus, or at least recognizes himself to be in the presence of God himself. Again, Paul has argued, despite his own appreciation of the gift of tongues, to a preference for the gift of prophecy in Corinth.

Further Guidelines for Prayer Meetings

As Paul draws his discussion to a close, he again asserts that the ultimate norm by which gifts are used in public is the common good; to achieve this good, order must prevail. It is interesting to note, as Paul gives his concrete directives, that "each at the meeting should have something to share: a sermon, a song or psalm, a revelation, a gift of tongues, an interpretation of an expression of the gift of tongues" (14:26); there should be present "an interpreter of tongues, otherwise a person with the gift of tongues should use it only for himself" (14:27–28). The prophetic spirit, unlike the spirit involved in the speaking in tongues, can be halted in necessary situations; it should be halted, if someone suddenly receives a revelation (14:30–33).

That prophetic speech can be halted (or even saved for a later meeting) seems to be just a mild observation meant to help put order into the Corinthian prayer meetings, but verse 36 shows a certain shortness on Paul's part as though the prophets, too, must be causing some upset in these meetings and need to hear some of his authority.

Paul concludes the discussion begun in Chapter 12 with what he considers a fair norm: esteem the gifts of the Spirit, but do all in order and with propriety. A Christian prayer meeting is, then, governed by the good it can produce for the community, not by the pride an individual can foster by the misuse of a gift so that it becomes a typically pagan frenzy which does nothing but bring some kind of false admiration to the practitioner.

Verses 34 and 35, in which women are told "to remain quiet" at the Christian prayer meetings, deserve some particular comment.

Some people argue, with a certain reasonableness, that Paul never wrote these verses and thus, if they are odious, blame is not to be attributed to Paul. Other people will argue that, if certain words are taken in a certain way (e.g., the Greek word for "speak" should here be understood as "prattle" or "chatter"), Paul is not asking for total silence, but silence from useless banter. I would prefer a third way.

First, I think Paul is clear enough in distinguishing between women who pray publicly and prophesy, on the one hand, and, on the other, women who speak in ways less germane to the nature of the prayer meeting; I assume the Pauline authorship, therefore, of both these two verses and verse 5 in Chapter 11. Second, in the greater context one sees the obvious restrictions Paul is placing on a number of people, even people who have "a right" to speak because they are exercising true gifts of the Spirit; this includes not only those who speak in tongues, but prophets as well, men as well as women. Third, the treatment Paul gives to the gift of tongues is perhaps less than what one might like this valuable gift to receive. But it is evaluated against another norm here, namely what is the best way to save a quickly deteriorating community, and found to need its limitations exposed. Similarly, anything else which at the moment Paul senses is a threat to the community harmony is to be met with directness and even severity, even though in less dangerous circumstances he would pay it little or no attention. Fourth, in searching for a norm for establishing order, a norm which to him would serve best at least as a stop-gap measure, Paul here, as he did in the case of the covering of women's heads with veils, appeals to the custom "in all the churches." This norm, further, has the backing of "the law," which is presumably the Mosaic law, which never actually forbids women speaking in synagogues, but the broad interpretation of which did separate men from women in prayer. Thus, Paul appeals to a religious or cultural practice assumed from Judaism into the Christian communities by Jewish converts; Paul appeals to it as the most satisfactory of solutions offered to him at the moment.

In short, my own sense of what has transpired at Corinth and provoked this letter from Paul is a sense of such a threat to the community's very existence that prudential judgments are being made by Paul which are demanded by the need to save unity but might well be different in other circumstances. The decision here about women speaking at prayer meetings (not about their praying aloud or prophesying), as well as the firmness and shortness of temper behind it, looks to this very pressing need of the moment.

Indeed, Paul's last remarks (vv 39–40) reveal his norm in all the matters to be resolved as regards community prayer: keep and cherish what is good, but above all let everything be handled in orderly fashion and with propriety. Personal "concerns" and "manners" must yield to what is good for the group as a community; here this means orderliness, which is the effect of that which outstrips all other blessings: love.

STUDY QUESTIONS

1. Explain what unity exists among the diversity of the charisms of the Holy Spirit.

2. Why is pomposity inconsistent with possessing a charism?

3. Explain the body of Christ as it helps clarify the purpose of a charism.

4. Explain Chapter 11, vv. 2–3, as they relate to the problem of charisms.

5. Relate charity to the gifts of the Spirit. Why is charity "the most excellent way"?

6. Why is Paul reasonable when he limits the exercise of the gift of tongues?

7. Why is the gift of tongues valuable? Why is its value limited?

8. How do you explain Chapter 14, vv. 20–25, as they relate to Paul's argument about speaking in tongues prophecy?

9. What is to be thought of Paul's restriction on women in Chapter 14, vv. 34–35?

12

Tenth Problem:
The Misunderstanding
about Christian Resurrection (15:1–58)

In the judgment of many scholars, Paul saved the most significant problem for last; it is the question concerning the resurrection of the believer from the dead, and specifically the resurrection of the body. Indeed, from all we know from Paul's teachings ("his gospel"), the resurrection from the dead is absolutely essential to Christianity; Paul rarely cites the words of Jesus or his teachings and never speaks of his miracles, but his total attention is focused on the death and resurrection of Jesus and their significance. All meaning for the believer's happiness is contained in them, and so it is not surprising that Paul writes an extended answer to perplexities regarding this central belief.

Paul begins his discussion with a reminder—it is a reminder concerning the good news which saves, provided one believes as Paul has taught; to believe anything else leads to nothing. It is clear from these initial words how central Paul considered his role of mediator of the truth about salvation to be; this awareness of his role explains so much of his involvement and authority in the lives of the Corinthian Christians.

What is this reminder concerned with? What is "this gospel" which his readers need recall? It is the resurrection of the Lord Jesus from the dead which they must recall. We have not yet met directly the problem Paul received from the Corinthians, but are rather in the introduction to it, an introduction which Paul considers vital to the

15 Now I would remind you, brethren, in what terms I preached to you the gospel, which you received, in which you stand, [2]by which you are saved, if you hold it fast—unless you believed in vain.

3 For I delivered to you as of first importance what I also received, that Christ died for our sins in accordance with the scriptures, [4]that he was buried, that he was raised on the third day in accordance with the scriptures, [5]and that he appeared to Cephas, then to the twelve. [6]Then he appeared to more than five hundred brethren at one time, most of whom are still alive, though some have fallen asleep. [7]Then he appeared to James, then to all the apostles. [8]Last of all, as to one untimely born, he appeared also to me. [9]For I am the least of the apostles, unfit to be called an apostle, because I persecuted the church of God. [10]But by the grace of God I am what I am, and his grace toward me was not in vain. On the contrary, I worked harder than any of them, though it was not I, but the grace of God which is with me. [11]Whether then it was I or they, so we preach and so you believed.

12 Now if Christ is preached as raised from the dead, how can some of you say that there is no resurrection of the dead? But if there is no resurrection of the dead, then Christ has not been raised; [14]if Christ has not been raised, then our preaching is in vain and your faith is in vain. [15]We are even found to be misrepresenting God, because we testified of God that he raised Christ, whom he did not raise if it is true that the dead are not raised. [16]For if the dead are not raised, then Christ has not been raised. [17]If Christ has not been raised, your faith is futile and you are still in your sins. [18]Then those also who have fallen asleep in Christ have perished. [19]If for this life only we have hoped in Christ, we are of all men most to be pitied.

20 But in fact Christ has been raised from the dead, the first fruits of those who have fallen asleep. [21]For as by a man came death, by a man has come also the resurrection of the dead. [22]For as in Adam all die, so also in Christ shall all be made alive. [23]But each in his own order: Christ the first fruits, then at his coming those who belong to Christ. [24]Then comes the end, when he delivers the kingdom to God the Father after destroying every rule and every authority and power. [25]For he must reign until he has put all his enemies under his feet. [26]The last enemy to be destroyed is death. [27]"For God has put all things in subjection under his feet." But when it says, "All things are put in subjection under him," it is plain that he is excepted who put all things under him. [28]When all things are subjected to him, then the Son himself will also be subjected to him who put all things under him, that God may be everything to every one.

29 Otherwise, what do people mean by being baptized on behalf of the dead? If the dead are not raised at all, why are people baptized on their behalf? [30]Why am I in peril every hour? [31]I protest, brethren, by my pride in you which I have in Christ Jesus our Lord, I die every day! [32]What do I gain if, humanly speaking, I fought with beasts at Ephesus? If the dead are not raised, "Let us eat and drink for tomorrow we die." [33]Do not be deceived: "Bad company ruins good morals." [34]Come to your right mind, and sin no more. For some have no knowledge of God. I say this to your shame.

35 But some one will ask, "How are the dead raised? With what kind of body do they come?" [36]You foolish man! What you sow does not come to life unless it dies. [37]And what you sow is not the body which is to be, but a bare kernel, perhaps of wheat or of some other grain. But God gives it a body as he has chosen, and to each kind of seed its own body. [38]For not all flesh is alike, but there is one kind for men, another for animals, another for birds, and another for fish. [40]There are celestial bodies and there are terrestrial bodies; but the glory of the

celestial is one, and the glory of the terrestrial is another. [41]There is one glory of the sun, and another glory of the moon, and another glory of the stars; for star differs from star in glory.

42 So is it with the resurrection of the dead. What is sown is perishable, what is raised is imperishable. [43]It is sown in dishonor, it is raised in glory. It is sown in weakness, it is raised in power. [44]It is sown a physical body, it is raised a spiritual body. If there is a physical body, there is also a spiritual body. [45]Thus it is written, "The first man Adam became a living being"; the last Adam became a life-giving spirit. [46]But it is not the spiritual which is first but the physical, and then the spiritual. [47]The first man was from the earth, a man of dust; the second man is from heaven. [48]As was the man of dust, so are those who are of the dust; and as is the man of heaven, so are those who are of heaven. [49]Just as we have borne the image of the man of dust, we shall also bear the image of the man of heaven. [50]I tell you this, brethren: flesh and blood cannot inherit the kingdom of God, nor does the perishable inherit the imperishable.

[51]Lo! I tell you a mystery. We shall not all sleep, but we shall all be changed, [52]in a moment, in the twinkling of an eye, at the last trumpet. For the trumpet will sound, and the dead will be raised imperishable, and we shall be changed. [53]For this perishable nature must put on the imperishable, and this mortal nature must put on immortality. [54]When the perishable puts on the imperishable, and the mortal puts on immortality, then shall come to pass the saying that is written:

"Death is swallowed up in victory."

[55]"O death, where is thy victory?

O death, where is thy sting?"

[56]The sting of death is sin, and the power of sin is the law. [57]But thanks be to God, who gives us the victory through our Lord Jesus Christ.

> 58 Therefore, my beloved brethren, be steadfast, immovable, always abounding in the work of the Lord, knowing that in the Lord your labor is not in vain.

resolution of their difficulty. For the entire belief of the Christian in his own resurrection from the dead is totally dependent on the truth that Jesus rose, and bodily, from the dead. Without the latter in place, the former will not happen and makes no sense. Thus, to Paul's way of thinking, he must begin his response about the Christian's resurrection by affirming the resurrection of the Lord.

Paul reviews what he taught the Corinthians: Christ's death for sins, his burial, his resurrection from the dead—and a death and resurrection in accord with the Hebrew scripture. Paul recites a list of trustworthy first-generation Christians, ending with himself—all these have seen the risen Jesus. It is interesting how Paul interweaves, even for those who believe, the "proofs" of the resurrection with the reality itself: true burial, the witness of the scriptures, the eye-witnesses to the resurrected Jesus. The Acts of the Apostles uses the same three "proof-elements" (with "burial" involving "empty tomb") in call to belief in the risen Jesus. We are no doubt here in contact with elements of the earliest mode of presenting the Jesus-event: death, yes, but death for the sins of the audience; death confirmed by true burial, which prepares the way for the perplexing empty tomb; resurrection from the dead "on the third day," a phrase which shows that the resurrection has already been understood as fitting the Old Testament "third day" theme of God's glorious intervention; deep respect for Cephas (first) and the Twelve, as well as for James (not one of the Twelve).

Linking himself to the illustrious list of early Christians causes Paul to digress for a moment; he conveys the idea that, even though he was not "one of them," his teaching is as trustworthy as theirs (and, by implication, so is his authority).

Having put in full view the resurrection of Jesus with the "proofs" the Corinthians have known and accepted, Paul is ready to take up the question put to him about the resurrection of the Christian from the dead. He handles it in two steps: first, the fact of resurrection from the dead; then, the question of bodily resurrection.

The Resurrection of the Dead

Paul offers a number of arguments or considerations regarding the resurrection of Christ and the Christian; these are contained in verses 12 through 34. The first argument, which I believe Paul thinks to be his most significant, is subtle and asks for some comment; it falls between verses 12 and 19. The argument is formulated this way: if there is no resurrection from the dead, Christ is not risen; if Christ is not risen, there is no resurrection from the dead.

In one sense, under the aspect of pure logic, it follows that, if the statement is universally true that "there is no resurrection from the dead," then there is no room to affirm the resurrection of an individual from the dead; conversely, if one did rise from the dead, then it cannot be excluded that others rise from the dead, too. Thus, logically, the Corinthians cannot hold to a belief that Jesus rose from the dead, while asserting the universal statement that "there is no resurrection from the dead."

But I suspect that this logical approach is making too little of the problem of the Corinthians. I sense that they think they have not put themselves into a logical contradiction, but rather consider Jesus' resurrection from the dead to be an exception, to be of another order and outside the limits of what ordinary human beings can and will experience. This is what it means to call Jesus "Lord"; he is singular in essential ways, and the resurrection from the dead is one of them. I think this is what the Corinthians were suggesting in their belief in Jesus risen and denial of their own resurrection; and I believe that Paul's answer to them shows he is aware of their problem and answers it.

There are two possible ways by which to show that the Corinthians have misunderstood Jesus, and therefore his resurrection from the dead. First, though the Corinthians may well be right to consider Jesus in certain aspects singular and different from all other men, in the matter of the resurrection from the dead he is not singular and different. One must be able to distinguish between the elements in which Jesus is like us and the elements in which he is unique. Though Paul never makes a listing of these in letters we have from him, it is clear that he will not allow Jesus to be thought of as unique in the matter of resurrection from the dead. And though Paul does not explain the "how" of it, he affirms an essential link between the fate of Jesus and that of the believer.

But there is a second, and perhaps more perceptive way of explaining the "necessity" that, if Christ is raised, the believer will be raised as well. The argument is that Jesus was raised "for us," just as he is said to have died "for us." The force of the argument is that, just as Jesus would not have died if he had not died "for us," so he would not have been raised from the dead if he had not been raised "for us." But what does it mean that Jesus "is raised from the dead for us" if not that it is somehow through his resurrection that we will be raised to life? Thus, to affirm his resurrection, while denying its reason for happening and one of its major effects, makes no sense. If he rose, he must have risen *so that* we might rise. Thus, the Corinthians are denying an essential element of the significance of Jesus' resurrection, if they deny the resurrection of those who believe in Jesus.

Thus Paul is convinced, because Christ's resurrection is the cause of the Christian's resurrection and because the Christian shares the same destiny of eternal life with God as does Christ, that the person who believes in Christ must rise from the dead.

It is only logical for Paul to dwell on the immediate results of the viewpoint he is urgently opposing; if there is no resurrection of the Christian from the dead, then Christ has not been raised from the dead, which means that the preaching of Paul is useless, belief in that preaching is useless, Paul is a perjurer in that he swore before God that Jesus was raised, the Corinthians without Jesus risen remain with sins unforgiven, deceased Christians have really perished for they have no hope of rising from the dead. Such are the implications of the Corinthian statement that there is no resurrection from the dead for the believer. Indeed, Paul is right to conclude that the believer is the most unfortunate of human beings, if the believer's hope in Christ must center on this life only; not that the life which Jesus encourages the believer to live is unreasonable, but the hope that expects unending life from love is absolutely fruitless, for the Corinthians have denied the very possibility.

With verses 20 through 28 Paul turns to a positive type of argument, an argument wherein he shows the way in which Jesus' resurrection and that of the Christian linked to it answer the deepest problems of life; it is an argument of "fittingness," for the resurrection is the most fitting solution to the human condition. This condition which envelops all mankind is symbolized by Adam who, with his sin, consciously separated himself from God, and thereby separated himself from Life. All human beings share in this separation from Life, but union with the risen Jesus can overcome this definitive separation and offer mankind again the opportunity to live—to live with God.

As Paul describes the change in human destiny brought about by the risen Jesus, he begins to dwell on that reversal which, in the terms of Hebrew scripture, speaks of Christ as king over all powers which tyrannize human beings until the day when they will be totally subjected to him and he will present them, subdued, to the Father. At this time, everything will once again, purged from disobedience and submissive to God, be filled with the goodness and love of God, as full as is ever possible. It is the resurrection from the dead, Jesus' resurrection and then that of the believer, which is the entry-point to this everlastingness. For it is not just to live forever that is the deepest promise of the resurrection, but it is to live forever with God that all living things hope for; Jesus, for all his central role as the one who "died for our sins and rose for our state of justification," looks to the Father to fill the believers with the fullest godliness.

Another Dimension of Baptism

In his final remarks about resurrection from the dead, Paul continues to provide arguments in favor of belief in it. First, there is the practice, no longer maintained by most churches founded on Christ, that one could be baptized on behalf of someone who was already dead (and unbaptized). The idea behind this practice seems to have been this, that Christ's coming at a certain time in history surely did not cut off from the chance of salvation those who died just a few days or months or years before Jesus did, or just a short time before the preaching about him came to their town or city. (Such too was the thinking behind the idea that Jesus, after his death and before his appearance to the women at the tomb, visited the underworld to free all the friends of God from Adam to the time of the resurrection; time should not work against the offer of salvation.) Paul is showing the Corinthians that even their own practice of baptism for others contradicts their disbelief in the resurrection of human beings from the dead.

Earlier, Paul had argued that, if there is no resurrection from the dead, he perjured himself in swearing that Jesus rose from the dead. Now he argues that his whole life is meaningless, especially the immense suffering he has had to endure, if there is no resurrection from the dead. Presumably the "wild animals" Paul had to fight at Ephesus were people who opposed and persecuted him.

Finally, Paul alludes to the situation in Corinth that some of the believers, under the influence of lost hope in the life after death, recite the words Isaiah put on the lips of disbelieving Jerusalem in a moment of its forgetting God: "Let us eat and drink today, for tomorrow we die" (Is 22:13). These words reflect the deep distrust in God that his advice will assure Israel of continued life, despite the power of the enemy. Those who embitter the Corinthians about a life with God after death open the door to the discouragement that leads to all forms of grasping for whatever happiness one might think he can suck from this present life. The

Corinthians have come back to the very life without God that they had before Paul came to them; is not that very life an argument that there should be something better, a resurrection from the dead?

The Resurrection of the Body

Paul now moves on to the second major topic regarding resurrection from the dead, namely, the bodily resurrection. It is striking that in this section there is no reference to the body of the risen Christ, though it might have been expected from the way in which Paul began this chapter. Why is there no mention of Christ's body? The answer underlines the difficulty Paul is faced with and the seriousness of the Corinthians' problem. Let us look for a moment at Christ's resurrection.

The great majority of pertinent texts of the New Testament, and especially of the Gospels and Acts of the Apostles, witness to the bodily resurrection of Jesus. The empty tomb is cited often as an indication of this, and Jesus' eating with his disciples, being touched by Thomas and held by Mary Magdalene contribute to this witness. It seems that every effort is made whether prior to Jesus' death (for instance, in his predictions about his suffering and resurrection) or afterward, to affirm that the person who died on the cross is fully risen, that nothing has changed essentially between the time of the crucifixion and the time of the resurrection. Jesus' resurrection serves as a model for that hope the disciples have for their own resurrection, and yet Jesus' physical resurrection is not argued by Paul as a point in favor of the physical resurrection of the disciples. The reason for this seems to center on the time difference between the death of Jesus and his resurrection, on the one hand, and on the time lag between the death of the believer and his resurrection, on the other. Jesus is reported dead about 3:00 P.M. on a Friday afternoon and was seen risen near sunrise of Sunday; since no one actually saw the resurrection take place, it cannot be denied that Jesus lived again physically even before Sunday sunrise. The clear implication of this is that the body of Jesus had little time to corrupt, if indeed it was to corrupt at all. This is not the condition of the disciple. In fact, given the known conditions of many of the corpses of the believers, one could only conclude that Jesus' physical resurrection had little in common with whatever physical resurrection one should assume for the disciples. Indeed, pondering the fate of the various bodies of the deceased believers inevitably forced the serious question: no matter how God did it with Jesus, how will he make rise again a body which has decomposed or even in a decomposed state been scattered by the winds of fortune? What does physical resurrection, in these cases, mean?

There are three arguments in favor of bodily resurrection; two are explicitly cited in Paul's letter, specifically between verses 35 and 53, and a third is what I will suggest as an influence on Paul from the Old Testament, an influence which is real though not explicitly mentioned here. Let us look at these three points.

Aspects of Bodily Form

The bulk of Paul's argument is centered on the principle that each form of life or existence has its own physical form; the physical form is dictated by the kind of existence it will enjoy. This is evident in the case of wheat, which has one physical form before it is put into the ground and another when, the grain having "died," the wheat rises out of the ground. This first of Paul's examples is very well chosen, for it involves not only the physical form's changing to suit the new state of existence, but the passage of "burial in the ground" in order to reach the new state of existence.

But much of nature argues the point Paul is making; everything has a physical body suited to its existence, its role, its nature. It is true of birds and animals, it is true of the heavenly bodies. One should therefore be able to understand that one will have one kind of body while living in this life, in this age, but a different kind of body in the next life, a body which is suitable to the state of existence which is characterized by imperishability, glory, power, spirit—all qualities which are not characteristic of "this age."

Paul, appealing again to the figure of Adam, draws out more fully the difference between Adam and us, on the one hand, and Christ and the Christians, on the other. As usual, Paul begins with a text of the scripture; this time it is from the Book of Genesis, where it is said that God breathed life into the man and he "became a living soul" (Gen 2:7). It is the Greek translation of the Old Testament which speaks of man as a living "soul," a description which corresponded to the anthropology/psychology of Paul's world which acknowledged that man was made up of three distinguishable principles: body, soul and spirit. With scripture Paul, therefore, defines man as a living soul while a participant in this age, but must indicate what distinguishes man in the age to come; this he does by showing that Christ, the source of the Christian's new existence, has gone from being a living soul to being a "life-giving spirit." It is this "spirit" which man will be given, a spirit whereby he will live the new life, for the spirit is "life-giving." In this way, human beings, who were modeled on the source who was Adam, will be modeled on the new source, the source of life in the new age, Christ. Each age, then, dictates what physical form is to be had as proper for it. The age to come is the age in which God will be all in all; that is, the Spirit, which enlivens the risen Jesus, will be the Spirit communicated to the believer to bring him alive. With such a difference between the age characterized by Adam and his descendants and that of the "life-giving spirit," one can only expect that the body will be fitting to the new form of existence.

The Limits of Flesh and Blood

This exposition by Paul brings him to his second, more limited argument: that flesh and blood cannot inherit the kingdom of God. This theme, which is strongly developed in other New Testament works, argues to the absoluteness of the chasm which separates existence in this world from that with God in his world. In hope that this new world will come soon, Paul imagines that not everyone will be found dead at the time this world is to cease. But not to die does not mean no change; all must change, for it is impossible that one live in the next age with the qualities or characteristics fitted to this age.

Behind these ideas of Paul regarding the physical resurrection there seems to be an implicit assumption about human existence, whether in this age or in the age to come, which is drawn from the Hebrew scripture. To put it another way, why would Paul be so insistent on the presence of the body in the next life, if he can only describe it rather generally and if he could apparently get by with a concept of the self glorified and alive in the Spirit, but without the body? Indeed, for many Greek philosophers of Paul's time, the body is symbolic of all that changes, that brings corruption, that interrupts contemplation of the good; if the self moves to a new life, why would it be at all desirable to be burdened again by a body which only makes demands on the soul?

As a Pharisee, Paul had believed in a resurrection from the dead; Jesus' resurrection, therefore, served to confirm something in which Paul already believed and clarified its causes. Not only was resurrection of the dead to be the interpretation of many texts of the Old Testament, but there was something of a speculative underpinning to this belief which would help make sense of the texts, and which suggests why Paul was so tenacious in his belief before the Corinthians. For this we must go back to Genesis.

Support from the Old Testament

In the first creation story (Gen 1:1–2:4), God made man and acknowledged that what he had made was "very good" (Gen 1:31). In the second creation story (Gen 2:5–25), that which God has called "very good," the man, is the entire entity which he holds in his hand;

it is the "dust of the soil with the breath of life breathed into it." This entire thing, dust and breath of God, is very good. But if God has called it all "very good," how would it be possible that he would, when the time comes to save man, save only part of that which is "very good" and not all of it? It seems to me that this might well have been the kind of witness scripture gave whereby Paul should be led to hold so firmly to a view which was neither very popular among the Greeks nor at all easy to imagine or describe. But it seems absolutely essential that the whole person be saved and filled with the Spirit; God would not let an essential element of a person called "very good" escape the grace of re-union with God. Indeed, though Jesus' resurrection does little to explain the physical resurrection of the believer from the dead, it is itself the witness that the gracing of the entire person is God's saving intention.

For all its difficulty to explain and imagine, Paul insists that existence in the age to come will be a "total" existence, the fullness of humanness enlivened by the Spirit of God.

Paul has answered the questions of the Corinthians about the resurrection from the dead, the physical resurrection. He cannot but move from the mode of teaching to the mode of enjoyment of the teaching. He cites the prophet Isaiah who says that death is swallowed up by being conquered (Is 25:8), and then, with the notion of "conquered" still in his mind, he adapts a quotation from Hosea which joyously notes that death has no victory, no sting (Hos 13:14). Oh yes, people will die, but that is not victory for death. One can speak only of a victory for death, if death really keeps one dead. What kind of victory is it if, after one dies, one returns to life? That is like a bite which has no sting. Death's real victory is to keep one dead, and Christ has ended that kind of victory. In that sense, those who are in him will never die.

STUDY QUESTIONS

1. What is the problem Paul faces concerning resurrection from the dead? Why is Jesus' resurrection the first thing Paul mentions when he addresses the Corinthians' problem?

2. Explain Paul's sentence, "If Christ is not risen, there is no resurrection for anyone; if there is no resurrection from the dead, Christ is not risen."

3. What logically follows, in Paul's way of thinking, if Jesus did not rise from the dead?

4. How, by Jesus' resurrection from the dead, do Jesus and the Father repair the failing of Adam?

5. What is the Corinthian problem about the resurrection of the body of a believer? How is this problem answered?

13

The Letter's End (16:1–24)

Many letters of the first century A.D. end with a number of scattered thoughts and information after the main theme or themes have been handled at length in the body of the letter; so it is with this First Letter to the Corinthians. Paul's first remarks have to do with a collection of money which he tirelessly encouraged and gathered for years on behalf of the impoverished churches in Israel. One reads about Paul's concern for this collection of money in a number of his letters; perhaps the most famous passage showing Paul's long-term commitment to this collection occurs in his recollections written in the Letter to the Galatians, where he notes that James, Cephas (= Peter) and John shook hands with Paul and Barnabas, as a sign that they would be partners but would go to the pagans, "insisting on only one thing, that we should remember to help the poor, as indeed I [= Paul] was anxious to do" (Gal 2:10). And one gets the flavor of Paul's concern for money-raising through the entire Chapters 8 and 9 of the Second Letter to the Corinthians. What is noteworthy in Paul's remarks in the First Letter to the Corinthians is the plan whereby one puts aside "each Sunday" something which will eventually be brought to Jerusalem and Paul's careful wording so that he does not give any impression of avarice or self-interest in the gathering, handling and delivery of the money to Jerusalem.

Paul's second interest is in his making known to the Corinthians his planned itinerary insofar as it affects them and his coming to visit them. It seems that Paul would like to arrive in Corinth for this projected visit at the latest sometime in the fall; thus his words "staying with you, perhaps even passing the winter with you" (16:6) make

16 Now concerning the contribution for the saints: as I directed the churches of Galatia, so you also are to do. [2]On the first day of every week, each of you is to put something aside and store it up, as he may prosper, so that contributions need not be made when I come. [3]And when I arrive, I will send those whom you accredit by letter to carry your gift to Jerusalem. [4]If it seems advisable that I should go also, they will accompany me.

5 I will visit you after passing through Macedo'nia, [6]and perhaps I will stay with you or even spend the winter, so that you may speed me on my journey, wherever I go. [7]For I do not want to see you now just in passing; I hope to spend some time with you, if the Lord permits. [8]But I will stay in Ephesus until Pentecost, [9]for a wide door for effective work has opened to me, and there are many adversaries.

10 When Timothy comes, see that you put him at ease among you, for he is doing the work of the Lord, as I am. [11]So let no one despise him. Speed him on his way in peace, that he may return to me; for I am expecting him with the brethren.

12 As for our brother Apol'los, I strongly urged him to visit you with the other brethren, but it was not at all his will to come now. He will come when he has opportunity.

13 Be watchful, stand firm in your faith, be courageous, be strong. [14]Let all that you do be done in love.

15 Now, brethren, you know that the household of Steph'anas were the first converts in Acha'ia, and they have devoted themselves to the service of the saints; [16]I urge you to be subject to such men and to every fellow worker and laborer. [17]I rejoice at the coming of Steph'anas and Fortuna'tus and Acha'icus, because they have made up for your

absence; [18]for they refreshed my spirit as well as yours. Give recognition to such men.

19 The churches of Asia send greetings. Aq'uila and Prisca, together with the church in their house, send you hearty greetings in the Lord. [20]All the brethren send greetings. Greet one another with a holy kiss.

21 I, Paul, write this greeting with my own hand. [22]If any one has no love for the Lord, let him be accursed. Our Lord, come! [23]The grace of the Lord Jesus be with you. [24]My love be with you all in Christ Jesus. Amen.

sense. Moreover, it seems that the earliest Paul would arrive in Corinth would be only early summer, for he will remain "in Ephesus until Pentecost," which occurs sometime in May or early June. Such words, expressing at the most an intention and a certain vagueness of execution, perhaps became the knot of contention which Paul had to untie in his Second Letter to the Corinthians, where he answers a huffy criticism that he has not come to Corinth as he had said he would, and thus showed his lack of devotion to the Corinthians. What the "great and promising door" was which was to open up new areas for missionary work is not clear. Perhaps it is a reference to Rome and even areas beyond that; this would coincide with the statement of Luke in the Acts of the Apostles at Chapter 19, verses 21–22, where an itinerary, similar to the one given in the First Letter to the Corinthians, is indicated: from Ephesus through Macedonia to Achaia (= Greece), wherein lies Corinth, then Rome.

Paul always shows great concern for those who do work like his and great appreciation for those who help the missionaries along. Thus, his third interest in these concluding verses is to encourage the Corinthians to receive Paul's co-workers generously and to honor those who have helped these preachers.

It seems to me that the reference at verse 17 to the arrival of certain Corinthians at Paul's side indicates that this letter of Paul was almost finished when these three men came to him; perhaps they calmed Paul's mind as to some of the problems which he is addressing because of the news he received from earlier groups of Corinthians.

Finally, Paul renews greetings to the Corinthians, those of the churches of Asia (i.e., today's Turkey), which includes the major center of Ephesus, those of Aquila and Prisca (short for Priscilla) whom one meets in the Acts of the Apostles (18:18,26) and in the Letter to the Romans (16:3), those of a number of brethren and, finally, his own.

The last lines of this letter contain some information of more than passing interest. The concept of the "holy kiss" is traceable back to the first century A.D. among Christians in letters like this; the liturgical greeting of peace is a particularized form of this sign of Christian love. Paul sends a greeting by writing his own name— a sign which suggests that most all of the previous letter was dictated. This raises the question about the vocabulary and style of the letter, for dictation need be only thought of as generally giving ideas and leaving the formulation of them to the secretary. Most scholars would prefer, however, to think of Paul as intimately involved in the very terminology of the letter, even if he had a secretary for it.

Paul also wishes a curse upon those who do not love the Lord. This rather formidable attitude toward these people is perhaps a remnant of his extreme Pharisaism which encouraged those who were faithful to God to keep separate from those who were not and which ultimately led some Pharisees to consider hating God's enemies a virtue. The wish for a curse furthers, of course, the separation of the Christians from those who could undermine their new faith; it makes things black and white for Corinthians who saw only gray. Finally, Paul repeats the now long-established formula, drawn from the liturgy: "Come, Lord [Jesus]." Quoted here in Greek letters, it is really from the language of Palestine and thus rooted in the earliest church tradition. It reveals already so early the belief that Jesus deserves the title "Lord," and it signals the burgeoning outlook of hope that characterizes the Christian—the hope that what was begun in Palestine will be brought to completion with the return of the Lord. It forces one to focus on the horizon of life and not simply on the memory of Jesus in early Palestine. One need not have been a companion of Jesus in Nazareth to have enjoyed the salvation he intended to bring; for that salvation is still to come, and all those who believe in him will share in it, for from their hearts rises the cry for him: Come, Lord! It is, finally, a confession of faith in that it acknowledges that it is Jesus to whom the speaker is committed and on whom the speaker counts for all happiness.

Paul ends his letter with the assurance of his love; it is a sign that all that he has written was motivated by this love and need be understood that way. What he has written, then, is for their good, as he sees it, now. It is within this love for them that they should measure his words.

Study Questions

1. What concerns are on Paul's mind as he closes his letter. Explain these concerns.
2. Explain "holy kiss," the implications of Paul's calling attention to his writing "in his own hand," the sentence, "Come, Lord (Jesus)."